Understanding
Yourself
and
Others™
Series

DYNAMICS OF PERSONALITY TYPE

Understanding and Applying
JUNG'S COGNITIVE PROCESSES

Linda V. Berens

LEARNING • PROBLEM SOLVING • COMMUNICATING

Telos
PUBLICATIONS
Huntington Beach, California

D1264961

PRINTED IN THE UNITED STATES OF AMERICA

Published By:

Telos Publications, a division of Temperament Research Institute
P.O. Box 4457, Huntington Beach, California 92605-4457
714.841.0041 or 800.700.4874 / fax 714.841.0312
www.telospublications.com / www.tri-network.com

International Standard Book Number: 0–9664624–5–9

03 02 01 00 99   10 9 8 7 6 5 4 3 2 1

Cover Photo: Fallen Leaf
© 1998 Jim Brandenburg/Minden Pictures, used with permission.
Cover/Layout Design/Illustrations: Kristoffer R. Kiler
Illustrations: Chris Berens of Thumbnail Productions, Austin, Texas

ORDERING INFORMATION

Individual Sales U.S.: This publication can be purchased directly from Telos Publications at the address above.
Individual Sales International: Please contact Telos Publications at the address above for a list of international distributors.
Quantity Sales: Special discounts are available on quantity purchases by corporations, associations, and others. For details contact Telos Publications at the address above.
Orders for College Textbook/Course Adoption Use: Please contact Telos Publications at the address above.
Orders by U.S./International Trade Bookstores and Wholesalers: Please contact Telos Publications at the address above.

TRAINING AND CONSULTING INFORMATION

Individual Training: Training is available for further exploration of the information provided in this book. Please contact Temperament Research Institute at the address or telephone number above for a full curriculum schedule.
In-House Training and Consulting: Temperament Research Institute provides in-house training for communication, team building, leadership development, coaching, and organizational development.
Facilitator Training: Temperament Research Institute is an approved provider of Myers-Briggs Type Indicator® (MBTI®) Qualifying Programs. TRI also provides train-the-trainer workshops for temperament and The Self-Discovery Process™.

Acknowledgments
Thanks to the following people: (listed in order of first appearance in the development of this book)
• David Keirsey for making me aware of the consequences of speaking about processes as if they were "parts" and "homunculi" operating on their own.
• Katharine Myers for helping me see that Jung's descriptions were about processes and your supportive dialog ever since.
• Stephanie Rogers for joining with me in doing things a different way and keeping my values in front of me.
• Margaret Hartzler for creating a space for innovation and your focus on the eight processes.
• Gary Hartzler for hours of dialog and argument in the quest for enlightenment and clarity.
• John Beebe for new ideas and a conversation about how the "place" in the hierarchy influences how the processes look.
• Linda Ernst, Melissa Smith, and Judy Robb for helping me blaze the trail as we found ways to communicate about Jung's cognitive processes so people don't get confused.
• Dario Nardi for hours and hours and hours of conceptualizing, critiquing, editing, differentiating and pushing the boundaries of my thinking. Thanks also for sharing your own ideas so freely and helping me organize and put words to mine. Without your help, this book would not yet exist.
• Fritjof Capra for giving me a language for talking about Jung's functions consistent with systems thinking.
• Kris Kiler for pushing me to get this book written and for helping me know what is important and how to communicate it.
• Steve Myers for also focusing on Jung's functions and for challenging me to examine my assumptions.
• Vicky Jo Varner for such enthusiastic support and coming to the rescue at the last minute!

Thanks to the following people for giving so freely of their time to help us have balance in the descriptions of the processes: Chris Berens, Lynne Berens, Eric Conant, Gary Ernst, Linda Ernst, Kris Kiler, Stephanie Kiler, Judy Lind, Dario Nardi, Greg Sawyer, Marci Segal, Melissa Smith, Sola Power, and David Specht. Because of you we were able to filter through all eight processes in all eight positions.

Thanks also to participants in our classes who "test drove" the book as pre-work for their MBTI Qualifying program and to Dario Nardi's students who used the descriptions in their own self-discovery. You helped us know it works.

About the Author

Linda V. Berens

Linda V. Berens, Ph.D. is the Director and Founder of Temperament Research Institute, which provides organizational consulting, training and MBTI qualifying programs. She is the author of *Understanding Yourself and Others™: An Introduction to Temperament*, and coauthor of *The 16 Personality Types: Descriptions for Self-Discovery*, and *Working Together: A Personality Approach to Management* as well as numerous training materials. As an organizational development consultant, she applies systems thinking and understanding individual differences to solving organizational problems. She is a licensed Marriage and Family Therapist and Educational Psychologist, and has over twenty-five years experience using temperament and type with individuals and teams and teaching these theories to professionals. Linda is recognized internationally for her contributions to the field of psychological type, for integrating temperament and Jung's typology, and for developing user friendly training materials for practical application of those theories.

Contents

A Word from the Author

Why I wrote this book

I have found a deeper understanding of type dynamics and the cognitive processes is indispensable when I work with individuals who truly want to find their best-fit type pattern. I always use this information in the background to facilitate accurate self-discovery, but we needed a tool for practitioners to use directly with clients to make it available and understandable to them as well.

I also saw a need for descriptions that would reflect the many ways each cognitive process may be observed, not only when it is a dominant process. I wanted descriptions of each process to reflect its most positive aspects in both its active modes and passive modes. I wanted these descriptions to include examples of less developed uses of each process. And I wanted descriptions that would lead to holistic systems thinking rather than a mechanistic parts model approach.

Now, more than ever, people need to know themselves and to explore ways to grow and develop, rather than leaving it up to chance. I wanted to make the concepts of type dynamics and type development available and useful to people who want to learn more about themselves for their own self-leadership.

I hope to share some insights gathered in my twenty-five years of work with this theory. There is much in this book that is "cutting edge." It represents an integration of my reading of Jung and conversations with leaders in the type field, as well as many years of observing type, talking about type, and helping people discover their best-fit type pattern.

Design

This booklet is designed to guide the reader through a self-discovery and self-exploration process. We aim to meet the needs of a variety of learning styles, and incorporated graphics, personal anecdotes, activities, a conceptual overview, theoretical frameworks, practical examples, and inspirational quotes to achieve that end. Some of the brief descriptions of the type patterns in their learning and problem-solving mode reflect more than just the cognitive processes because we wanted to help unguided, novice readers begin to identify themselves.

We also included an appendix written for the type knowledgeable to explain how and why we have departed from a traditional approach to explaining type.

History

Early in my career as a user of the MBTI®, I became frustrated by having to present the dichotomies separately, and then later seeing people confused about which preference accounted for what behavior. As I grew in my understanding of what the four-letter code really stands for, I wanted to help people comprehend the meaning of type dynamics and development.

Also as I was teaching professionals to use the MBTI, I found I was spending hours helping them "crack the code" of the MBTI, but they still did not grasp how it represented a dynamic pattern. So in 1994, I spontaneously introduced participants to Jung's functions in a different way. I began by stating briefly that we have a world inside us and a world outside us, and we can look at what we do in each world. Then I guided them through briefly experiencing the cognitive processes by directing their attention and engaging them in each process right on the spot. After that, I pointed out that the J and P at the end of the code indicated which process they are likely to use in the external world. I explored the dichotomies some more, and then we moved on to exploring the whole type pattern. Later, when I had to teach them to figure out the dominant, auxiliary, tertiary, and inferior, they understood the concepts very quickly. They didn't have to unlearn anything! I've been doing self-discovery workshops this way ever since—first teaching temperament, then interaction styles, then the cognitive processes.

How to approach this book

With an open mind and ready to participate! We realize some readers will not care to do all of the many self-reflection activities. However, to gain the most from this booklet, please at least read through them, since useful concepts are expressed in the questions. And please let me know what works for you and what doesn't.

My best to you on your journey of deepening your understanding of yourself and others.

Linda V. Berens
December 1999

Personality in Everyday Life

We usually go about our lives without thinking about why or how people do things. Then when something isn't going well, we pause and ask, "Why are they doing that?" Even less often do we ask, "Why am I doing that?" or "Why did I say that?" We are so used to looking for tangible, black-and-white answers, we seldom ask, "How am I doing that? How am I approaching this problem?"

In our rush to find a simple solution or something or someone (even ourselves) to blame, we look for a cause. In the last century, people have focused on several "causes" for learning problems, interpersonal problems, conflict, communication difficulties, and even highly dysfunctional behavior. Maybe our gender makes us the way we are. Maybe it's our brain. Or perhaps it's the way we were raised. Such musings are natural, and the more complex our lives get, the more we feel the need to find a "cause." We need some semblance of order and control.

> If only we could understand what is behind what we do, we could find a way out of habitual patterns.

In everyday life, we do things for different reasons. We have habitual ways of doing and thinking about things. These habitual ways are influenced by our inborn tendencies as well as our life experiences.

Since the 1980s, the general public has become used to looking at personality in terms of various models of "personality type." And yet something seems to be missing. People say, "I don't want to be put in a box" or "I'm a little of all of these" or "Don't we change over time?" This booklet seeks to give you a better understanding of your "personality type" and its various dynamics.

> I really don't want to be put in a box. I want some tools for adapting and solving problems.

Philosophers and scientists have been sorting people and their behaviors into categories for over twenty-five centuries. For many people, some of the typologies "speak" to them, explaining why they do what they do and validating that they are "normal" and okay just the way

they are. Personality typing can certainly help us understand someone else's perspectives so we can get along better and communicate more effectively. Yet there is more to personality than just categories and boxes. There are also the various dynamics of personality type—our natural mental processes that have movement and "energy flow" and are constantly taking in and evaluating information.

Personality in Everyday Life Is Dynamic

To look at the dynamics of personality type, we need to look at the processes we use in our everyday lives—ways we go about doing things.

> I want a road map to help myself and others with our development.

We must understand that we are dynamic—adaptable and responsive to the needs of the moment. We are constantly developing—growing and evolving in relation to the demands placed on us.

Everyday life involves communicating, learning to do new things or to see things in a different way, and solving problems and making decisions.

- What determines how you learn best?
- Why is learning easier at different points in your life?
- What are the processes involved in any decision?
- What determines how you are likely to approach a problem?
- What kinds of decisions do you make easily and effortlessly? What kinds are hard?
- What kinds of information make the most sense to you? What kinds confuse you and make you work harder to understand?

> I want something useful that can show me what to do differently to make things better.

Dynamics of Personality Type

What Is Personality?

Over the years, philosophers and behavioral scientists have been trying to find ways to understand what they call personality. Personality has many meanings, and different views about personality come from different assumptions about why we do what we do. Before we can understand the whys and hows of what we do and then use that understanding, we need to recognize the different assumptions we have about personality.

The many theories of personality can be understood in terms of how they attribute "cause" to behaviors.

The Causal Matrix
Assumptions about Why We Are the Way We Are

	The Individual	The Environment
Free Will	We are free to determine our own behavior based on our mental models and our belief systems.	We are free to determine our own behavior based on the roles we play in our interactions with others.
Determined	Our behavior is determined by what we inherited or was imprinted on us in early life.	Our behavior is determined by the responses we get from the external environment.

Actually, all of these perspectives are true. We like the definition of personality given by Salvatore Maddi.

Personality is a stable set of characteristics and tendencies that determine those commonalities and differences in the psychological behavior (thoughts, feelings, and actions) of people that have continuity in time and that may not be easily understood as the sole result of the social and biological pressures of the moment.*

A History of Personality Type

In the 1920s, the idea of personality type was being explored by leading scientists and philosophers. A Swiss psychiatrist, Carl Jung, wrote *Psychological Types* during that time, in which he gave a detailed description of what has now become one of the most widely used typologies in the world. His theory of psychological type has sparked more than one personality inventory and an international membership organization of professionals and lay people alike devoted to deepening their understanding of typology and its competent and ethical use. A multitude of Internet sites and e-mail lists center around this typology.

> *"The Self is our life's goal, for it is the completest expression of that fateful combination we call individuality."*
> **—Carl Jung**

The Basics of Jung's Theory of Psychological Types

As Jung was trying to understand the differences between the viewpoints and approaches of his colleagues Sigmund Freud and Alfred Adler, he realized they focused on different worlds. Freud seemed to be focused on the external world of adjustment to the outside world as he approached his patients, and Adler seemed to be more focused on the primacy of the patients' inner world in determining their behaviors. Following this realization, Jung defined his fundamental concepts of the *extraverted* and *introverted attitudes*. He declared that some people orient themselves primarily to the world outside themselves and are thus *extraverted* in their natures. These people are energized by interaction with the outer world. On the other hand, others orient themselves more readily to the world inside themselves and are *introverted* in their natures. They are more energized by solitary, reflective activities.

Functions—Cognitive Processes

After observing people through the lens of extraversion and introversion for a while, Jung came to realize that it wasn't just an orientation to the inner world or outer world that made people different from each other. It was also important to consider what mental activities they were engaging in when they were in these worlds. Jung called these mental activities *functions*, based on the "function" being performed. Now they are frequently referred to as mental or *cognitive processes*. Jung

---

* Salvatore R. Maddi, *Personality Theories: A Comparative Analysis*, 3d ed. (Homewood, Ill: The Dorsey Press, 1976), 9.

described four cognitive processes and said that every mental act consists of using at least one of these four cognitive processes. Furthermore, these cognitive processes are used in either an extraverted or introverted way, making eight processes.

Perception

Jung classified the functions into two major groupings. He noted that there are two major kinds of *mental processes*. One is *perception*, a process of becoming aware of something. In the perceptive process, there is some sort of stimulation and we become aware of or attend to that stimulation. It is how we gather or access information. Jung called this an *irrational* process since the awareness simply comes to us. Jung identified two kinds of perception—*Sensation* and *Intuition*. Sensing is a process of becoming aware of tangible information. INtuiting* is a process of becoming aware of conceptual information. Sensing and iNtuiting can both be done in either the outer, extraverted world or in the inner, introverted world.

Judgment

The other kind of mental process identified by Jung is that of *judgment*, a process of organizing, evaluating, and coming to conclusions. Using the judging process, some sort of evaluation is made. Jung identified two kinds of judgment—*Thinking* and *Feeling*, both of which can be used in either the outer, extraverted world or in the inner, introverted world. Simply put, Thinking judgments are based on objective criteria or principles, and Feeling judgments are based on personal, interpersonal, or universal values.

Eight Personality Types

Jung described eight personality types, each characterized by a predominance of one of the four functions, used in either the extraverted or introverted attitude. His descriptions of the eight types in *Psychological Types* still ring true, and scholars are still referring to those descriptions to help them understand cognitive processes.

"It is often very difficult to find out whether a person belongs to one type or another, especially in regard to oneself."
—Carl Jung**

Along Came the MBTI

In the 1940s, Isabel Myers began developing a self-report questionnaire that could help people find where they fit in Jung's theory. Her mother, Katharine Briggs, had been exploring Jung's typology since the late 1920s. She was interested in its applicability to fiction writing as well as helping people understand their differences. As Myers and Briggs began to craft a self-report instrument, they faced several challenges. They had to take what Jung had seen as an integrated whole and try to figure out how to ask questions to get at that whole. They chose to focus on Jung's notion of opposites and force choices between equally desirable, psychological opposites.

Opposites

Jung understood the functions to be dichotomous opposites. Dichotomous opposites are like a pencil with an eraser. The use of one is opposite to the action of the other. Both uses are needed, useful, and equally valuable. Sensing and iNtuiting are opposite in their nature. You might say that you cannot attend to more than one kind of information at any one time. However, you can shift your attention from one kind of information to another and in fact do so many times. For example, you might notice the young, green leaves of a tree (sensory information) and then think symbolically of spring and new beginnings (intuitive information). Thinking and Feeling judgments are also opposites. To be value-based and criterion-based at the same time is impossible. However, in any given situation, both may be used. In prioritizing, for example, you may have some criteria to check for, and then you may consider what is important.

Myers and Briggs then faced the difficulty of how to find out which function was the dominant function. According to Jung, the goal is not to use all the functions equally well but to have one that is *dominant* or trusted and developed most. We can characterize a personality by describing the dominant process in its most polished, skillful, and elegant execution. Jung also indicated that there was more to a personality type than the dominant function. The dominant process gives a person only one mental process to rely on, and if the dominant process is a perceptive process (Sensing or iNtuiting), there would be no way to evaluate information, so there must be a preference also for a judging process. Likewise, if the dominant process is a judging process (Thinking or Feeling), there would be no way to access information. So the personality is also characterized by having another process play an *auxiliary* role that provides support to the dominant. The idea of a dominant and auxiliary is often referred to as the hierarchy of functions.

---

* We use Sensing and iNtuiting to refer to mental processes rather than sensation and intuition, which refer to names of something. Our focus is on the activity, not a person's "type."

** Carl G. Jung, *Psychological Types* (Princeton, N.J., Princeton University Press, 1995), 3.

Balance

The auxiliary process provides balance to the dominant process in two ways.

1. The kind of process, perception or judgment, is different. If the dominant process is a perceiving process, then the auxiliary process is a judging process or vice versa.

2. The attitudes or orientations of the processes are different. If the dominant process is focused on the outer world (extraverted), then the auxiliary process is focused on the inner world (introverted) or vice versa.

Revealing the Sixteen Types

In order to identify the patterns suggested by Jung, Myers and Briggs conceived of a fourth dichotomy that indicates whether someone prefers to live their outer life using a judging process or a perceiving process. This has come to be known as the Judging-Perceiving dichotomy. The reasoning was that if people live their external lives using their preferred judging process (Thinking or Feeling), they would be more likely to want to structure their lives according to a plan. If they live their outer life using their preferred perceiving process (Sensing or iNtuiting), they would be more likely to want to see what a situation brings and keep their options open for action.

The addition of this dichotomy made Jung's concepts more accessible to the general public and allowed the identification of sixteen personality types.

The Four-Letter Personality Type Code*

	COGNITIVE PROCESSES		
Your Preferred World	Preferred Perception Process	Preferred Judgment Process	Orientation to the Outer World
E or I	S or N	T or F	J or P

The "Magic" Type Code

Thus the Myers-Briggs Type Indicator® (MBTI®) was developed to bring Jung's theory to life. By answering some questions that force you to choose between two equally acceptable choices for everyday actions, the MBTI yields a four-letter code that points you to a personality pattern that reflects Jung's theory. This four-letter code has become a worldwide language for looking at differences. This simple process seemed magical. For many people, it made visible what had been invisible. For many, it gave value to heretofore unrecognized contributions and even legitimized their existence.

In the 1980s, personality tests began to be widely used beyond the psychologist's office. Type became popular. *Please Understand Me*, David Keirsey and Marilyn Bates' book on the twenty-five-century-old temperament theory, became a best seller. While it was based on a different model, it was linked with the MBTI and spread the language of type even further. More books were published by major publishers, not just type enthusiasts. Magazine articles were written. MBTI was becoming a "brand name."

Unintended Consequences

As the MBTI became more popular, the instrument became confused with the theory, so anything having to do with type was referred to as "MBTI." The dichotomies themselves (E-I, S-N, T-F, J-P) became the important aspect of type, and what the type code really stood for was frequently seen as too complicated to explain. Most practitioners forgot (or never even understood) that the Judging-Perceiving dichotomy was developed to help access the dynamics of the cognitive processes, not to label behaviors or people. The dichotomies took on a life of their own. Many forgot that the purpose of the instrument was to help people find their best-fit type pattern and instead fell into the seduction of the measurement mentality. People were allowed to believe that they were the type they "tested" as rather than encouraged to engage in a process of self-discovery.

> *"It is not the purpose of a psychological typology to classify human beings into categories— this in itself would be pretty pointless."*
> **—Carl Jung****

While psychological type remains popular and has spread across the world, working its magic for many people, there are pockets of backlash. In organizations where the use of the MBTI resulted in simplistic stereotypes, the theory has been rejected. More holistic, systems-thinking practitioners see type labeling as limiting growth and interfering with teamwork, rather than promoting it. The unintended consequences of making type simple are being felt. Many spin-offs that ignored the richness of the theory behind the model led to oversimplifications and labeling. As bullet-point lists with overly simplistic and imprecise descriptors were substituted for full narrative

---

* Please refer to Appendix B for a more complete resource for "cracking" the MBTI personality type code.

** Carl G. Jung, *Psychological Types* (Princeton, N.J., Princeton University Press, 1995), 554.

descriptions of whole types, "mis-identification" of type preferences occurred. The very bias that the MBTI was created to overcome crept back in. The dynamics and developmental aspects of type were rarely mentioned. Stereotyping became the result instead of the constructive use of differences that was intended by the developers of the MBTI.

Even before the backlash, some were going back to Jung's work to clarify definitions. Angelo Spoto commented on the worship of "the archetype of order." John Beebe focused on the possibility of the eight function-attitudes playing out in our psyches in archetypal ways. Many started teaching about the dynamics of personality type, and type development began to be emphasized.

Type as a Whole Pattern, Not Just Four Letters

The early developers of the MBTI never lost sight of type as a whole. The limitation of measurement methods and the parts model thinking of the era led to an artificial separation of the dimensions of type outlined by Jung. The organismic, Gestalt-Field-Systems view that lay behind his thinking has come back into the mainstream as the concept of living systems has become more widely embraced.

Now there is a trend toward understanding the type code as representing a pattern of how we use the eight cognitive processes: extraverted Sensing, introverted Sensing, extraverted iNtuiting, introverted iNtuit-ing, extraverted Thinking, introverted Thinking, extraverted Feeling, and introverted Feeling.

This book is designed to help you understand these processes as they play out in your personality, influencing your actions on a daily basis.

When the full meaning of Jung's theory of psychological types is considered, it becomes a theory that addresses all areas of the causal matrix.

The Causal Matrix
An Interpretation Using Jung's Model of Psychological Types

	The Individual	The Environment
Free Will	We develop and adapt. We are free to create our own character based on how we respond to life's challenges as well as our own unfolding pattern of development.	We are free to respond in our interactions outside our innate preferred pattern of responses. Each interaction can trigger unique responses using any one of the eight cognitive processes.
Determined	We have natural inclinations from birth. Included in the pattern of these natural inclinations is an unfolding pattern of development.	Responses from the environment can affect our behavior on an unconscious behavioral level. The more unconscious/unaware we are, the more likely we are to be affected in a stimulus-response kind of way.

What do you see yourself doing with your new understanding of yourself and the cognitive processes?

My goal for learning more about my pattern of cognitive processes is . . .

A Systems Perspective

Personality can be seen as a living system.

Humans are very complex and cannot be understood in terms of a few simple formulas. While interest in mental processes goes back at least to the early twentieth century, it lay dormant until the last half of this century. In the 1960s, Gregory Bateson highlighted mental processes as essential properties of systems. In recent years there has been a whole field of study called cognitive science. We tend to think of cognition as relating to the brain, yet it is a property of the whole person.

We are not mechanical systems that are "built." Rather, we are living systems that are dynamic and growing. There is no single "cause" of our behavior. There are multiple influences such as those in the causal matrix. A living-systems approach to understanding personality considers all of these influences. When trying to understand ourselves and others, it is helpful to have some simple, easy-to-comprehend principles to guide us. For example, Fritjof Capra* has said that to understand any "living system" you have to look at the pattern, processes, and structure of the system. To Capra's principles we add purpose.

Structure—the What

Structure refers to the physical expression of the system. Frequently this is what we see first. We often try to understand personality as if it is a fixed structure. This is how many people think of "personality type"— something solid and stable. In the case of personality, we may think of the concrete structure provided by the brain and the nervous system. Recent research shows patterns of brain activity related to personality differences, but this kind of information is not very useful to us on an everyday basis. It is also not the whole picture.

Pattern—Patterns of Organization

Pattern refers to the interrelationships within a system. Every system, including personality, is defined by essential characteristics. These are the qualities that must exist, such as the trunk, roots, or branches of a tree in relation to each other. More recently in our understanding of personality, we've begun to look at the pattern of characteristics that form our commonalities and differences.

Purpose

Purpose is revealed in the holistic theme of the pattern as it interacts with the larger system of which it is a member. Each cognitive process contributes to this purpose through its role in the personality type pattern.

Processes—the How

Processes are the activities the system engages in as it functions in day-to-day life and as it grows, adapts, and changes. They are best described using verbs that indicate actions. Processes are dynamic and changing. We can't examine processes directly. To understand them, we must look at the behaviors to see evidence of processes.

When trying to describe a process, we have to take into account movement over time. Processes are moment-to-moment and repeat in different sequences. When we try to look at a process, we "freeze-frame" it—we artificially stop and take a snapshot. Meanwhile, the system has moved on and is engaging in other processes.

No single process occurs in isolation.

Here are some examples of processes you might have used in deciding what to wear this morning:

- **Experiencing** (trying on) and noticing what else was in your closet.
- **Recalling** and remembering the last time you wore a particular outfit or the last time you were at a similar event—maybe even remembering how you felt then.
- **Inferring** and noticing the possible meanings of what you might wear: "Wearing this communicates…"
- **Envisioning** yourself in an outfit or maybe even envisioning yourself being a certain way.
- **Organizing** the outfit according to criteria and consequences: "Since I have to stand all day…"
- **Analyzing** your options using principles like comfort or "red is a power color."
- **Considering** what would be appropriate for the situation: "One should or shouldn't wear…" or "People will think…"
- **Evaluating** whether you like an outfit or not: "This outfit suits me and feels right."

*For more on the theory of living systems, see Fritjof Capra, *The Web of Life: A New Scientific Understanding of Living Systems* (New York, N.Y.: Anchor Books, 1996).

Development, Growth, and Adaptation

Processes are the means by which we grow, develop, and adapt. Growth, development, and the ability to change are written in to our DNA, just as much as the consistency of our characteristics.

> Trees, like all living-systems, undergo a growth process that is "programmed" from the beginning. To know more about the growth process of a tree, we look at evidence of its effects on structure. As a tree grows, the structure is affected by the process as evidenced in the growth rings.

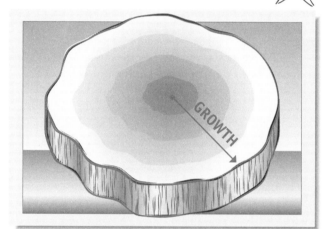

> Although the tree is "programmed" to grow straight and branch out on all sides, it can bend due to environmental influences like the direction of light.

Processes are both driven from within the system and influenced by the environment. We are "patterned" to behave in certain ways, yet we adapt to the environment.

The Nature of Processes

Processes have meaning only in reference to the whole context. When we look at these processes, they do not occur in isolation but in relation to each other and to the larger system.

> In the process of deciding what to wear, you might consider what's appropriate and what others like. This evaluation process could involve two different sources of information. One person might recall the last time the outfit was worn to use as an information source for the decision. Another person might visualize himself or herself in a new situation and think of how people are responding.

Finding Your "Self"

Patterns, processes, and structure are all interrelated. Aspects of each are used to help us understand, "measure," or map the system called "you." Sometimes we focus on discrete processes, sometimes on broad patterns, sometimes on narrower patterns. The whole is always there. Structure, pattern, and process are all present at the same time—we just shift our focus to serve our needs at the time.

When all of these measures intersect in the same "place," we can be more sure we have accurately described and can understand the *true self*.

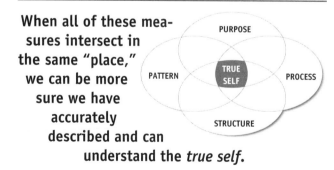

The process quality of personality makes it very difficult to measure. How can you be described in any definite and specific way since you are constantly changing, adapting, and evolving? You can take several snapshots from several different perspectives to get a more complete picture. Any single perspective will provide a rather limited view.

Understanding Your "Self"

We can view who we are in several ways. It is as if we have different "selves."

The Contextual Self

The *contextual self* is who we are in any given environment. It is how we behave depending on what the situation requires. Here is where our flexibility and adaptability come into play. We have the tools of the eight cognitive processes to help us adapt to the needs of the situation. The more skill and comfort we have with any one of them, the more likely we are to use that one in the context. However, a specific environment may require, push us to use, or even challenge us to become skilled at other processes.

The Developed Self

When the contextual self becomes habitual and ongoing, it becomes an aspect of the *developed self*. Several factors influence our development. First of all, our inborn tendencies have a natural way of unfolding and developing. Given our particular inborn pattern of using the cognitive processes, we are more likely to develop some of them at different times in our lives and even avoid or ignore others.

The responses of the environment as we engage with it can also subtly influence our development. If we get rewarded for certain behaviors and punished for others, we can't help but be influenced.

But we also make choices and decisions as we exercise our free will in response to what life presents us. And other people influence us through our interactions and roles.

The True Self

An aspect of our personality exists from the beginning of our lives. This aspect of ourselves is in our genes, our DNA. We are born with a tendency to behave in certain ways, which influences how we adapt, grow and develop. When we act in congruence with this *true self*, we are more likely to be in a state of "flow," of high energy. When we have to act in ways that are different

from our natural inclinations, we are likely to pay a high energy cost.

In understanding ourselves, it is important to understand all of these "selves" and to honor the ways we can be in all instances. It is important to not limit our self-knowledge to just our contextual self, our developed self, or our true self.

When we seek to understand our "self," we must realize that each of these "selves" could be quite similar to each other, or they could also be quite different from each other.

Understanding our Different "Selves"

In the case of differences, we might be using different cognitive processes as required by the context. This is one reason that trying to figure out the true self is difficult when we look at a single behavior. Another reason is that we may have adapted to life's challenges by suppressing some of our natural inclinations and by developing cognitive processes that are not part of our natural pattern. When these processes have become an integral part of our developed self, it is often very difficult to determine our true self.

When we use a personality instrument to help us, sometimes we answer the questions in terms of the contextual self, such as how we are at work. Sometimes we answer in terms of a developed self. It is important to realize that no one instrument by itself or a single view of personality will easily get at the true self. We have found that a variety of approaches, taken together, works best to help us understand our "self."

The Patterns of Processes

We can use all eight cognitive processes, yet we have preferences or natural inclinations for some of them. We are naturally inclined to use these eight processes in a pattern.

The pattern of our preferences for using the processes represents the way our minds are naturally organized. This pattern is not a combination of characteristics like colors mixed in paint or connected building blocks. The pattern of organization exists from the beginning. Our pattern of preferences is sometimes referred to as our personality type or *best-fit type*.

Finding Your *Best-Fit Type* Pattern

Best-fit type refers to the personality type pattern that you decide fits you best. No one description or pattern will be a perfect match to all of who you are. Your personality is rich and complex, and a "type" or type pattern cannot adequately express all of that richness.

Our Unique Patterns of Behavior

Our best-fit type predicts which cognitive processes we are inclined to use naturally. Yet we are free to use whatever "tool" works to meet the challenges of a situation. Since we have innate preferences, we are likely to respond more automatically using one or two of the tools. When we develop skill with the other tools, we are freer to use them. When we really develop a tool, it also becomes an aspect of our developed self, available to us without conscious effort. Here is where we get our uniqueness.

Sometimes people come to understand who they are through self-reporting on personality instruments. No instrument is completely accurate. A validation process, preferably involving self-discovery, must accompany all of them. Many instruments have standards that require face-to-face facilitated feedback with a qualified professional to help control for any measurement error and to assist in understanding and applying the information. The MBTI, for example, is one of those instruments.

If you already know the four-letter code that represents your best-fit type, you can use this booklet to understand more about how you function in the world. If you have not yet fully explored or identified your best-fit type, this booklet may help you in that process.

An instrument will not tell you who you are; it can only indicate who you might be. It will not tell you what you do or even can do; it can only predict what you are likely to do.

Self-Discovery

One powerful way to find your best-fit type pattern is through self-discovery. A process of self-discovery actively engages you in your own personality assessment. It helps you access your sense of self, which you can obtain only if you stop and listen to it. For self-discovery to work, you need to do the suggested activities and pay attention to how you feel as you participate.

Self-Reflection

We have found that identification of one's best-fit type is not easy when trying to identify one's preferences for the dichotomous processes. This is because day-to-day life requires us to use more than our preferences, and certain tasks, roles, and environments draw on different processes. To help you, we have presented several opportunities to reflect on how you use the cognitive processes in learning, problem solving, and communicating.

Interaction with Others— Sharing and Feedback

We can learn who we are through our interactions with others. Finding people who are similar to us and comparing notes and sharing stories helps many of us discover our own best-fit type pattern. One valuable way of finding out who we are is by actively seeking feedback—asking others to tell us how they see us. These people may be trained facilitators or merely people who know us well. And remember, this feedback is a gift, often given through the eyes of the giver—so seek feedback from many people.

Openness to New Information

During the process of self-discovery, "unconscious" information sometimes comes into our minds—aspects previously unknown to ourselves and others. The unconscious is often where we "store" information about how to "be" in the world. As you explore who you are, stay open to valuable insights from within yourself as well as from instruments and feedback.

Many variables may be involved in your self-discovery process. Be aware that family, social, cultural, and other influences will affect how you view yourself in relation to the type patterns. These influences are often unconscious until they somehow come into our awareness, when they can be described and pointed out. Stay open and searching until you find a good fit that feels right.

Four Easy Steps

1. Identify your own preferred learning pattern.
2. Experience the eight cognitive processes.
3. Apply the cognitive processes to your own learning, problem solving, and communicating.
4. Integrate your understanding and exploration to find your best-fit type.

Cognitive Processes and Learning

All eight cognitive processes play a role in our learning. We enter a learning situation with some perceptions already formed and some judgments already made. We are more open to certain kinds of information and more inclined to organize that information in certain ways.

> *"In times of change, learners shall inherit the earth, while the learned are beautifully equipped for a world that no longer exists."*
> —Eric Hoffer

> *"The will to learn is an intrinsic motive, one that finds both its source and its reward in its own energy."*
> —Jerome Bruner*

One way we use the cognitive processes in our daily lives is with learning. Learning is not just something we do in school or in formal settings. We learn every day. Sometimes our very survival depends on how well we can learn. That may mean unlearning our learned limitations and regaining confidence in our ability to direct our own learning.

What if we all could learn how we learn? Then if some kinds of learning were harder than others, we could find the source of that difficulty rather than rejecting what is being taught or feeling bad about ourselves for not learning.

Exploring Your Learning Experiences

Let's explore learning as a way for you to understand both your natural inclinations and the eight cognitive processes. Later we will look at applying your new knowledge to take charge of your learning.

> *"What the school imposes often fails to enlist the natural energies that sustain spontaneous learning—curiosity, a desire for competence, aspiration to emulate a model, and a deep-sensed commitment to the web of social reciprocity."*
> —Jerome Bruner*

In today's world, someone who doesn't know how to learn is left behind. By exploring your own learning process and determining your natural learning style, you can find the best ways for you to learn. Then you, not the instructor or the situation, are in charge of your learning.

Learning is broadly defined as change. The focus can be on what we learn (the product of learning) or on how we learn (the process). It is about how we change and how we adapt, grow, and develop. This adaptation, growth, and development occur from the inside out.

When we start where we are with who we are, we are then free to truly learn from the interactions we have with our environment.

You have had many learning experiences in your life. Some of them were good, some bad. Take a moment to recall the learning experiences you have had. Think in terms of your adult learning as well as when you were younger. Think also about your learning experiences that were not in school, especially when you learned easily and effortlessly.

*As quoted in Malcolm Knowles, *The Adult Learner: A Neglected Species* (Houston, Texas: Gulf Publishing Company, 1990), 91.

Your Best Learning Experiences

What made them the best?
What came naturally to you?
What skills were you learning?
What content were you learning?
What attitudes were you acquiring?

Your Worst Learning Experiences

What made them the worst?
What was difficult or "energy draining"?
What skills were you having to learn?
What content were you having to learn?
What attitudes were being changed?

Now read the following eight learning pattern descriptions on the next two pages and see which ones match your best and your worst learning experiences. These descriptions were developed from people's answers to the very same questions you just answered, so one or two of them will probably feel just right to you. You can start by skimming the bolded words and then read more in depth to find a good fit.

Circle how well each learning pattern description fits your natural learning style.

The Guide Learning Style

I learn best when there is consideration of the **ultimate goals and effects on others**, when I can set out to achieve something or acquire knowledge that is completely new to me but has some **relevance to the future**. I want the satisfaction that what I am learning will have direct significant applications and lasting impact for years to come.

The **attitude and enthusiasm of the teacher** is everything, and being inspired really makes a difference. I do much better when the teacher tries to connect with me, and feedback and coaching from my teacher motivate me the most. I like a learning environment that is open to differing perspectives and where my perspective is valued.

I like to be associated with a mentor or group of individuals with whom I can discuss ideas or projects on the relevant meaning or connections of what we are learning. I also like writing down my ideas to **share with others.**

I remember ideas best when given a chance to tie ideas together and make them **personally meaningful** with the opportunity to process the experience and material and **synthesize them into something new**. I love it when I am able to see an insight come to life.

Encouragement and positive feedback are essential, and I learn best without criticism—when there is cooperation, not conflict.

☹ 1   🙁 2   😐 3   🙂 4   ☺ 5

The Mediator Learning Style

I learn best when I can see the greater significance, what it symbolizes, in terms of my values and people. I like interaction. It gives me opportunities for lights to come on in my head; to **get insights about others and the deeper issues involved.** I like observing and being part of the learning.

I like having a **meaningful purpose** or goal, knowing what I want to achieve. I need to see the value in what I am doing or learning and that it is not superficial and uninspired.

Discussing new perceptions and the reasons why something is the way it is and why the information is important to what we are doing is something I like. Then I prefer to have minimum guidelines, so I can do what I want. I learn best when I don't have to worry about what the instructor wants.

Experiential learning applied to my own life with some component of **self-discovery** and development speaks to me personally.

Of course, I want the learning to be interesting. I enjoy learning anything I wouldn't normally be exposed to. I need to **relate ideas and concepts to my personal experiences**. Getting a feeling of growth and accomplishment is very important.

I need **friendly, enthusiastic, authentic feedback and encouragement.** I want to be recognized for my uniqueness and creativity.

☹ 1   🙁 2   😐 3   🙂 4   ☺ 5

The Coordinator Learning Style

I learn best when there is a **theory or rationale** behind learning something. Since I always have goals for self-improvement, I like being aware of the importance and the techniques to do something differently.

I like to **envision a concept**, a **system,** or solutions. Let me know I can use the learning to reach the cause of a problem and **go beyond it**, and give me models so I can "see" what I am learning. I like some degree of ambiguity so I can extend the concepts and learning process. I hate memorization and repetition and anything that's pointless.

I like **exploring a new topic on my own** before engaging in a group activity, and I work best when I am able to pursue an interesting area when it "hits" me. Let me watch someone do something well before I try it, but I usually have to learn a method at my own pace.

Insightful learning, with clear ideas grounded in research, substance, or exploration, is best. Of course, **credible "expert" delivery** is important. I **often think "but what if?"** and I need to test out ideas to check if they can work.

Successful implementation helps me see a concept in action and lets me know I have mastered it, and I like **acknowledgment of original ideas and objective feedback** for making improvements.

☹ 1   🙁 2   😐 3   🙂 4   ☺ 5

The Engineer Learning Style

I learn best when what we are trying to learn is addressed at the **conceptual** level, with **good models**. An inspiring concept with a solid framework and a clear objective holds my attention and makes it easy to hang on to and build upon. There has to be an intriguing body of **knowledge to master**. I also have to know why I am being asked to learn or do something, and there have to be theoretical justifications and explanations.

I want an **instructor who knows the subject well** and has new information. I want to be able to ask questions and to show I understand the content.

Knowing enough about something before the learning activity often helps, as does having time to think about what I am learning. Memorization or repetition is a turnoff. I prefer a setting that allows me to be creative and express myself while setting a challenge for myself. And articulate, bright peers give an **opportunity to discuss and exchange ideas and share insights**.

I prefer a **loose structure** with no strict agenda or schedule. This gives me a chance to process and discuss ideas to their logical conclusion. It also gives a chance to experience and experiment.

I usually don't need much feedback, but I may want **feedback from the expert** on the quality and accuracy of my performance or achievement.

☹ 1   🙁 2   😐 3   🙂 4   ☺ 5

Circle how well each learning pattern description fits your natural learning style.

The Monitor Learning Style

I learn best when I have a **sense of structure and a systematic approach.** Tell me why it works this way. It has to be applicable to my work and my life, not abstract. Give me a chance to know how something relates to other things I'm doing and learning.

I want to know the steps I have to take to be successful. Memorization, drill, and practice give me the experience I need. Writing down the steps often helps. **Structured learning and routine that makes sense** help. Show me the right way, and then give me support and guidance without looking over my shoulder all the time. Show me you believe I can do it.

A knowledgeable and **experienced instructor** who gives clear instructions and organized ideas is the best. Focus on the goal of helping the class learn. Make the assignments interesting and **reinforce what's being taught.** Be sure we are held accountable for the assignments and give us real-life examples that are logical and reasonable. Following through on questions in a timely manner is also helpful.

I need **concrete, behavioral feedback**—the sooner, the better, so I don't practice incorrectly. Give me some positive feedback first, then constructive criticism, so I can improve my performance.

☹   ☹   ☺   ☺   ☺
1   2   3   4   5

The Conservator Learning Style

I learn best when I know the goals and a **suggested way to proceed. Structure and routine also help me.** I want to find out how the system works, with explanations of "why" something fits where it is.

I learn experientially by asking questions during the learning process. I also enjoy sitting back and **listening to knowledgeable people** about things that are interesting, when that's appropriate, and generally I prefer cooperative games and stories about people that help make learning more real to me. It helps when the learning is applied to real life, with hands-on activities, where I am actually doing what I am learning. I will work hard on such activities, and I like to work my way through them, a bit at a time.

I like being **shown how to do something step by step.** I like to follow the step-by-step instructions a few times, then do it on my own. I don't mind memorizing and practicing when that's what's needed.

I learn best **when the instructor takes an interest in me** and my learning. I like an organized instructor who provides accurate materials. Fairness is as important as friendliness. A positive, enthusiastic environment helps, so I can get the reassurance I need to know I am doing the right thing.

☹   ☹   ☺   ☺   ☺
1   2   3   4   5

The Expeditor Learning Style

I learn best when there is a **combination of physical, concrete materials and broad principles**, so I can combine observations with logical principles. I want integration of evidence and theory focused on problem solving in a practical and useful situation.

Show me how learning this new thing will affect my future. Tell me the meaning and implications of my behavior. I want to know the immediate relevance and that there **will be an opportunity to use it.**

I learn best in an experiential way with **high participation, trying out several ways**, not just the "right" way. Situational learning with hands-on practice in make-or-break situations excites me.

Give me challenging, but not impossible, assignments. Let me experiment to get benefits or losses, depending on my decisions and actions. Keep it fast paced with minimal repetition and waste of time. **Games and competition make it fun.**

Unstructured environments with the freedom to explore different paths and not be confined by time and rules are important. Let me explore in my own way what interests me and what I find challenging.

☹   ☹   ☺   ☺   ☺
1   2   3   4   5

The Improvisor Learning Style

I learn best when I see the big picture up front, so I know what it's supposed to look like and what is **relevant.**

A good, supportive relationship with the instructor is as important to me as an interest in the subject. I need to **feel a sense of respect and patience from the person teaching me.** I like to have a chance to question things without feeling dumb.

I like learning **in order to accomplish something or help people**—like when there is a situation that requires me to gather resources—with the freedom to figure out what action to take.

I like knowing the context and how the subject relates to my experience. You can help me with clear direction of what to do with the material learned, good examples, and practical applications. Games make it fun.

I want a chance to **quickly apply** what I've learned and to try out the new knowledge right away. I really like it self-paced, so others don't slow me down.

I need **immediate feedback** to confirm the learning. I hate too much repetition and needless practice.

Learning is best when it is relaxed, challenging, and fun, but most important is the **freedom and independence to explore.**

☹   ☹   ☺   ☺   ☺
1   2   3   4   5

Cognitive Processes and Learning

<table>
<tr><td>

List the names of the two learning patterns that fit you *the best*.

</td><td>

List the names of the two learning patterns that fit you *the least*.

</td></tr>
</table>

We can look at learning using the lens of eight basic cognitive processes that contribute to and influence our learning. These processes have to do with how we access or gather information and how we organize and evaluate this information. Each of the preceding learning pattern descriptions reflects preferences for two of these processes: one kind of information-accessing process and one kind of evaluating process. We've described these processes below in terms of learning—how each contributes to learning and the kinds of questions most likely to be asked using that process.

Look at your learning experiences and learning style descriptions. Which of the processes are most prevalent in both your best learning and your worst learning experiences? Rank them in order of importance and appeal to you.

	Worst	Best	Rank
INFORMATION-ACCESSING PROCESSES			
Experiencing and noticing the physical world, scanning for visible reactions and relevant data What is really happening? What are the facts of the situation? What can I do with this now?			
Recalling past experiences, remembering detailed data and what it is linked to What have I already learned that I can build on? What resources and materials are available? What practical use does this have?			
Inferring relationships, noticing threads of meaning, and scanning for what could be What inferences can I make? What meanings am I perceiving? What hypotheses can I generate?			
Foreseeing implications, conceptualizing, and having images of the future or profound meaning What are the implications for the future? What are the concepts? What is the greater purpose?			
EVALUATING PROCESSES			
Organizing, segmenting, sorting, and applying logic and criteria How can I structure and organize my learning? What is the sequence and arrangement of what I am learning? What is the logic behind what I am learning?			
Analyzing, categorizing, and figuring out how something works What principles do I need to learn? What models can I fit the learning into? What techniques or approaches can I apply?			
Considering others and responding to them Who can I connect with, or relate to in order to learn better? Who can I help with this learning? How can I use this to improve my relationships?			
Evaluating importance and maintaining congruence What is really important here? What is of value to me, and what do I want out of this? Who is good to learn from?			

Let's explore Jung's theory of personality type further to see how these processes play out not only in learning but also in every aspect of our personalities. Then we will come back to look at your learning pattern and apply Jung's theory to helping you take charge of your own learning.

Jung's Cognitive Processes

A Language

It is helpful to have a language to use to describe the cognitive processes. The work of Carl Jung provides such a language. When Jung formulated his theory of psychological types, he felt he had found descriptors that covered the range of cognitive functions. The terms serve as metaphors that relate to our everyday experiences. Here are some basic definitions of the cognitive processes and how they relate to each other.

There Are Two Major Groups of Mental Activities

Perception	Judgment
Ways of accessing information	*Ways of evaluating*

There Are Two Kinds of Perception: Sensing and iNtuiting*

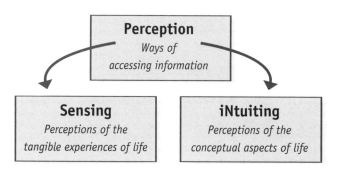

There Are Two Kinds of Judgment: Thinking and Feeling

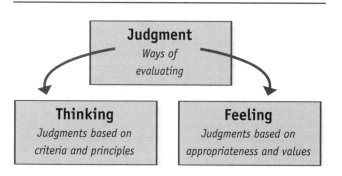

Already you probably have some common-sense idea of what these mean. The fact that the names relate to everyday actions makes them readily accepted as "true" as well as seem deceptively simple. As we explore the cognitive processes, we need to keep in mind that we are using the terms somewhat metaphorically and they have special definitions.

Perception

Perception is an active process. Both Sensing and iNtuiting are active processes where one's attention is drawn toward something, either inward or outward. Sensation is not just using the five senses. Intuition does not "build on" sensory information. Both kinds of information are always available.

Judgment

We have to abandon the usual meanings we give to the names in this category. Thinking as a cognitive process is not the same as thought, analysis, or intelligence. Here, it specifically means coming to decisions using objective criteria. Likewise, the Feeling process is not about emotion or feeling but about evaluating events and circumstances according to importance and values. Judgment is also an active process, and neither Feeling nor Thinking is merely passive.

Inner World or Outer World?

We can use these processes either in the world outside ourselves, the extraverted world, or in the world inside ourselves, the introverted world. When a cognitive process is extraverted, it has a different quality than when it is introverted. Thus the four basic mental processes described by Jung each have two expressions, which yields eight cognitive processes.

In this sense, these terms do not apply to personality "traits." Extraverted doesn't mean outgoing, talkative, or friendly. Introverted doesn't mean shy. Jung described extraversion and introversion as general attitudes which encompass patterns and tendencies, not "traits." In relation to the cognitive processes, we use these terms as indicators of the area of focus for a process.

> *"We then discover that no individual is simply introverted or extraverted, but that he is so in one of his functions."*
> **—Carl Jung****

* We use *Sensing* and *iNtuiting* to refer to mental processes rather than *sensation* and *intuition*, which refer to names of something. Our focus is on the activity, not a person's "type."

** Carl G. Jung, *Psychological Types* (Princeton, N.J., Princeton University Press, 1995), 519.

What Fits?

"The four processes—sensing, intuition, thinking, and feeling—are gifts that all people are born with. . . . It is up to each person to recognize his or her true preferences . . ."
—Isabel Briggs Myers*

As you reflect on your best and worst learning experiences, read the following descriptions of the cognitive processes. Use this worksheet to help clarify which processes you use most. Write down words or phrases that fit you—for those processes that come naturally and for those that don't—from the descriptions you have just read.

The Cognitive Processes Matrix

	e—Outer World Here and Now	i—Inner World Past, Future, Universal
Perception — Sensing	S_e extraverted Sensing	S_i introverted Sensing
Perception — iNtuiting	N_e extraverted iNtuiting	N_i introverted iNtuiting
Judgment — Thinking	T_e extraverted Thinking	T_i introverted Thinking
Judgment — Feeling	F_e extraverted Feeling	F_i introverted Feeling

*Isabel Briggs Myers with Peter B. Myers, *Gifts Differing: Understanding Personality Type* (Palo Alto, CA: Davies-Black Publishing, 1995), 193.

A Quick Guide for Observing Processes

When we look at any one aspect of a living system such as a pattern or process, we are seeing only a part of a larger picture. Here are some guidelines on how to observe processes and keep from getting them confused with structures and patterns.

Dichotomous Opposites

- There are various ways to view the cognitive processes as dichotomous opposites. The processes seem to be about the same kind of activity, yet they are opposite in the approach taken. We have a tendency to overuse some, and neglect their opposites.

Look-Alikes

- While the cognitive processes are different from each other, they also have aspects in common with each other. Some of the processes look alike in several ways, so we have included some of these on page 45.

Experiences from the Past

- It is easier to notice processes after they have happened, so reflect on how you have done things in the past. Then, with practice, you can learn to observe them while they are happening.

Look for Clues

- You don't see the process itself; rather, you see clues or evidence of the process. The clues are not the same as the process itself. This is like looking at the rings on a tree to see how the growth process occurred. The rings are not the same as the process.

Verbs, Not Nouns

- Remember that processes are activities. Use verbs to describe them, not nouns. Like verbs, they sometimes can be active and sometimes more passive.

Moment to Moment

- Remember that processes occur over a time period. We do not stay engaged in one process for a long duration but rapidly move from using one to another.

Notice Changes

- Observing processes requires that we notice differences, change, and variation. To better understand the cognitive processes, it will be helpful to compare and contrast them with each other.

Broad Categories or Clusters

- Jung's cognitive processes are categories of related activities that cluster together. You might consider the names of the processes as descriptive of themes. Remember, there is great variety in the expression of the processes.

Compare with Others

- Take a guess about which process was operating, then check out the evidence. Also check against the "expert opinion" of several experts, not just one. With Jung's cognitive processes, there is some disagreement, even among experts, about the definitions of the processes. The definitions that follow were developed after much reading of Jung's work and the literature on his theory, years of observation, and hours of discussion and debate. People who know themselves well were also asked to verify the fit of the descriptions. There was an attempt to describe the active forms of the processes as well as the more passive forms—ways we use them powerfully and less refined examples.

Sometimes trying to see which processes you habitually use is like noticing the air you breathe. It is always there, taken for granted and unnoticed.

Have Fun!
Enjoy the process of exploring the processes! As you do, try them on for size. See which ones are comfortable and easy to wear. Then see which ones you might want (or need) to develop.

The Cognitive Processes of Sensing

Sensing is a process of becoming aware of sensory information and often involves responding to that sensory information without any judgment or evaluation of it. Sensory information is concrete and tangible in nature. In the Sensing process, the focus is on the actual experience, the facts and the data. As an active perceptual process, it is more than stimulation of the five senses. It is the registration of that stimulation and actively being drawn outward to the concrete realities of a situation or inward to recollections of familiar experiences.

Extraverted Sensing (S$_e$)

> Look at the drawings of apples. Notice the shapes, the shadings, the placement on the page. Just allow your eye to go wherever it seems to "want" to go. "Stay with" the perception. (Don't jump to finding meaning, analyzing, or categorizing yet!)

When Sensing is directed outward, toward the external world, it is called extraverted Sensing (often coded as S$_e$). For example, you might look out your window and notice the apple tree in your backyard—the contrast of the ruby red apples and the deep green leaves, the rich brown-gray of the trunk and branches, and how the sunlight plays across the yard. You go out the door, reach out, pick an apple, and bite into it with a crunch, savoring the tree-ripened sweetness and the aroma of a really fresh apple. Sitting down on the ground, you feel the coolness under you and the warmth of the sun.

The Philosophy of Life That Engages Extraverted Sensing:

There is always more to be experienced, and opportunities don't last.

Examples of extraverted Sensing:

- Lenore was beside herself with joy as she played with the puppies in the pet store. She seemed to enjoy just being with them, petting them, making them jump up.

- In designing the ad on the computer, Mark kept trying different colors and changing the fonts, finding different ways to change the look. He was so absorbed in the page on the screen, he lost all track of time.

- As John experienced his first earthquake, he noticed the books "walking" off the shelf. Later he read in the newspaper that it was a 5.9 magnitude quake and the epicenter was only ten miles from his home. He read the whole article until he had all the facts, then he went to his computer and looked up even more statistics on earthquakes.

You are one with the experience. There is no "naming" or describing—just pure, vivid experience. The whole scene comes into your awareness almost at once. You may be drawn to experience more and more, seeking any variation that will intensely excite the senses. Writing that is richly descriptive can also evoke extraverted Sensing as can other mental stimulation. The process is momentary and tied to the events of the immediate situation. It occurs in the here and now and helps us know what is really there in the physical world and to adapt to it.

Extraverted Sensing occurs when we scan for information that is relevant to our interests, then we mentally register data and facts such as baseball statistics, the locations of all the restaurants in town, or the names of all the actors in the popular television shows. There can be an active seeking of more and more input to get the whole picture until all sources of input have been exhausted or something else captures our attention. Associated behaviors include eating a whole box of chocolates for the variety of tastes; playing an instrument for hours with pure enjoyment, not for practice; voracious reading; or continual asking of questions to get specifics.

ACTIVITY

Take a moment and look around you. Notice the smells, the sounds, the sights. What sounds do you notice in the background right now? Touch something and feel its texture. Focus on the variety of stimulations, allowing yourself to become absorbed in them. If something "excites" the senses, stay with that as long as it lasts.

Introverted Sensing (S$_i$)

> Look at the apple drawings on this page and allow a memory of apples to come to mind. Perhaps you can smell apples or an apple pie cooking—maybe even get a taste in your mouth. What feelings or feeling-tone came with the recollection?

If you were to look out your window and see an apple tree and immediately recall an image of an apple tree you've seen before and you were then aware of the feel of autumn in the air (even if it is late summer) and remember being in an apple orchard picking apples, you would be engaging in a process of introverted Sensing (coded as S$_i$). Your attention and energy would be turning inward; you would have disengaged with the outer sensory world and entered into the inner world of stored impressions. You might even tap into a series of memories and related sense impressions so that your mind seems to have traveled back to another time and place. Or you might recall a whole string of related historical data. Anytime you have an experience where you access information from those stored images, you engage in introverted Sensing. Using this process, we focus on the past, often bringing the past into the present. Sometimes there is a strong sense of "this is how it has always been and always will be." This process often provides useful information for planning for the future.

NOTE

Introverted Sensing is as real, concrete, and tangible as extraverted Sensing. Both can be active processes or can be experienced more passively.

The Philosophy of Life That Engages Introverted Sensing:

There is always a comparison to be made, and if it is familiar it is to be trusted.

Examples of introverted Sensing:

- Lenore's sister kept saying how much the standard poodle looked like the one they had as children. She said it reminded her of being at home and being young again.

- Robert had that look again. Jane knew he was going to resist her suggestion. He did it every time he had that wrinkle in his forehead.

- May knew the earthquake was different from the last one. For one thing, the last one left her queasy. This one had more of an up-and-down motion. She remembered the last one was a 4.3 magnitude quake.

Introverted Sensing often involves storing data and information, then comparing and contrasting the current stimulation with similar ones. The immediate experience or words are instantly linked with the prior experiences and one registers that there is a similarity or a difference—for example, noticing that some food doesn't taste the same and is saltier than it usually is. Introverted Sensing is also operating when you see someone who reminds you of someone else. Sometimes the feeling-tone associated with the recalled image comes into your awareness along with the information itself. Then the image can be so strong, your body responds as if reliving the experience. This could be seen as a source of feelings of nostalgia or longing for the way things were. In one instance, a young couple living in Europe spent their weekends trying out restaurants looking for food that tasted like American food.

ACTIVITY

Now as you look around, allow something you see to trigger an image of something you've experienced before and let the recollections flow for a while. Pause and notice how far afield you are from the external stimulus that started the recall.

Which fits you? As you read and reflect on the two ways of using the cognitive process of Sensing, does one feel easier and more comfortable? When accessing sensory information, which mode are you more likely to use or to trust more?

● **extraverted Sensing or introverted Sensing** ●

The Cognitive Processes of iNtuiting

Intuiting is a process of becoming aware of abstract information, like symbols, conceptual patterns, and meanings. It is an intangible "knowing" of what something means, how it relates to something else, or what might happen. Some call this the "sixth" sense. Sometimes this process is "triggered" by an external event, or sometimes this abstract information just seems to present itself to our awareness.

Extraverted iNtuiting (N$_e$)

Why do you suppose we chose apples to use as a stimulus for these activities? Brainstorm as many ideas as you can and make them as far-fetched as possible.

When the iNtuiting process is directed outward, it is called extraverted iNtuiting (coded as N$_e$). Let's go back to the apple tree outside the window. Using the cognitive process of extraverted iNtuiting, you might wonder why the former owner of your house planted an apple tree and why this kind of apple tree. Then you might consider why this kind of apple tree grows well in this climate but not in others. Or maybe it occurs to you that your life is like this apple tree in so many ways. Then you might become curious if apples represent the same ideas in other cultures and so on. Or you may even wonder, "What if the apple tree didn't exist?" When you find yourself letting your mind wander endlessly through thoughts that cannot

The Philosophy of Life That Engages Extraverted iNtuiting:

There are always other perspectives and new meanings to discover.

Examples of extraverted iNtuiting:

- During their conversation, Lenore suddenly recognized that the real reason her sister wanted a dog was because she was trying to replace the affection from her late husband.
- During an evening business class lecture, a student was so energized by connections to what she was doing in her job, she stayed up until 2 A.M. mind-mapping possible applications and ventures to present to her boss the next day.
- May wondered why the last earthquake left her queasy and seemed to affect her more, even though it wasn't as strong. She guessed it might have something to do with where she was standing at the time and the different motion involved. Or maybe she was more fatigued then.

be said, developing hypotheses from data, or inferring the meaning of something, you are engaging in extraverted iNtuiting. Using this process, we tune in extemporaneously to a multitude of possibilities and potentials. This helps us understand shifting relationships and meanings and be responsive to them as they occur.

Extraverted iNtuiting involves seeing things "as if," with various possible ways of representing reality. Using this process, we can hold many different ideas, thoughts, beliefs, and meanings in our minds at once with the possibility that they are all true. This is like weaving themes and "threads" together. We don't know the weave until a thought thread appears or is drawn out in the interaction with a previous one. Thus there is often an emergent quality to using this process. A strategy or concept emerges based on the here-and-now interactions, not appearing as a whole beforehand.

Extraverted iNtuiting involves realizing that there is always another view. An example is when you listen to one friend tell about an argument and understand perfectly and then listen to another friend tell a contradictory story and understand that view also. Then you wonder what the real story is because there are always so many different possible meanings.

ACTIVITY — Look around you and allow something you see in your environment to trigger a new idea or possibility. Or think of someone in your life right now and remember something he or she said or did recently or a look on someone's face. What do you suppose he or she means (meant) by that?

Introverted iNtuiting (N$_i$)

The Philosophy of Life That Engages Introverted iNtuiting:

There is always a future to realize and a significance to be revealed.

Examples of introverted iNtuiting:

- Lenore was thinking about the dog she and her sister were going to get when she got a flash of a dog barking and crying. Then she "knew" they needed to get a dog that didn't mind being alone.
- Noel was preparing for a workshop and had an idea to use a house to represent a certain personality pattern, a tree for another, books for another, and a target for another. These metaphors turned out to have universal recognition in almost every culture.
- Right after the earthquake, John suddenly knew that one day he would be a scientist studying phenomena like earthquakes.

> Think about apples. Allow yourself to quietly reflect on the way apples are symbolic of where you are in your life right now. The quieter you get, the more likely some universal meaning will come to you. (Be patient. We don't get much training in this kind of process in our society.)

If you looked outside your window and didn't even notice the apple tree that is there but instead got a sense that the orchards around will soon be cut down and replaced with a housing development, you would have experienced introverted iNtuiting. Introverted iNtuiting (coded as N$_i$) often involves a sense of what will be. The details might be a little fuzzy, but when you tune in to this process, there is some sense of how things will be. Using this process, we often are able to get pictures about the future or at least a sense of what will happen before we have any data. Sometimes it is an awareness of what is happening in another location and we have no sensory data to go on. Other times introverted iNtuiting operates when we conceptualize and get a sense of a whole plan, pattern, theory, or explanation. These are the kinds of images that come to us in the shower, in meditative states, or in dreams and help us deeply understand

something. Sometimes they are profoundly symbolic and even universally so. In using this process, we tune into a likely future or something universal. This information can then be used to decide what to do next, what to plan for.

Introverted iNtuiting involves synthesizing the seemingly paradoxical or contradictory, which takes a problem or situation to a new level. Using this process, we can have moments when a completely new, un-imagined realization comes to us. There is a disengagement from interactions in the room, followed by a sudden "aha!" or "that's it!" kind of experience. These kinds of experiences are often seen as if they are "psychic" in nature. The sense of the future and the realizations that come from introverted iNtuiting have a sureness to them and an imperative quality that seems to demand action.

ACTIVITY

Look around you again and allow yourself to be triggered into realizing the implications of doing something with an object you see. (Again, be patient. A perception of the future may not come quickly; just be alert to its subtle presence and it will surface.)

NOTE

Introverted iNtuiting and extraverted iNtuiting are not processes that "build on" sensory information. They are ways of accessing abstract information that may or may not have a direct relation to concrete and tangible events. Sometimes when we use either of these processes, we "justify" the information to a world that wants more tangible evidence by giving it the related concrete and tangible events.

Which fits you? As you read and reflect on the two ways of using the cognitive process of iNtuiting, does one feel easier and more comfortable? When accessing intuitive information, which mode are you more likely to use or to trust more?

● **extraverted iNtuiting or introverted iNtuiting** ●

The Cognitive Processes of Thinking

Thinking is a process of evaluating and making judgments based on objective criteria. Using this process, we detach ourselves from our values and seek to make decisions based on principles. Activities like discriminating according to a set of criteria or objectively defined standards, analysis according to a set of principles, logic, and cause-effect reasoning are all examples of using the cognitive process of Thinking.

Extraverted Thinking (T$_e$)

> Think about those apples again. As you notice the apples, how might you sort them?

Extraverted Thinking (coded as T$_e$) involves a process of putting order on the outer world according to either the principles inherent in what is being organized (like color, size, or shape) or some conventional order that is agreed upon (like alphabetizing or numbering). If you were to look outside at the apple tree in the backyard and notice the fruit was starting to fall off the tree, you might make a mental note to get several containers to put the apples in. You'd have a trash can handy for the rotten ones and a basket for the ripe ones to wash and put on the table. You'd also have a plastic pan for the ones that are bruised, but not rotten, to cut up for applesauce. Coordinating, sequencing, segmenting, and prioritizing often rely heavily on the process of extraverted Thinking. It has a more here-and-now quality than a universal, future, or past quality. When the particular events are out

The Philosophy of Life That Engages Extraverted Thinking:

Everything can be logical, structured, and organized.

Examples of extraverted Thinking:

- Lenore listed criteria she and her sister needed to match in selecting a dog. She wanted to be sure the dog didn't need a lot of attention since they were not home during the day. They lived in an apartment, so it was only logical it should be a small dog that didn't bark much.
- George broke down a task into smaller ones, thought of who had the time and skill, assigned the work, and scheduled a follow-up meeting. He also developed a backup plan for illnesses and other unexpected events so he could make sure the deadline was met.
- Even though John's own house was severely damaged in the earthquake, he got started on a plan to address problems at the local school. He drew up a schedule of professionals for helping with the impacts of the earthquake. He coordinated debriefing sessions with the teachers and the principal, and contacted the trauma counseling team to set up family meetings.

of our presence or awareness, the extraverted Thinking process reorients to the new data, event, or situation. This process often gives us some control over a situation, especially when everything is efficiently organized in a hierarchical manner.

Contingency planning, scheduling, and quantifying utilize the process of extraverted Thinking. Extraverted Thinking helps us organize our environment and ideas through charts, tables, graphs, flow charts, outlines, and so on. One woman labeled the shoeboxes for her 100 pairs of shoes for color, height, style, and comfort.

Sometimes the organizing of extraverted Thinking is more abstract, like a logical argument that is made to "rearrange" someone else's thinking process! An example is when we point out logical consequences and say, "If you do this, then that will happen." In written or verbal communication, extraverted Thinking helps us easily follow someone else's logic, sequence, or organization. It also helps us notice when something is missing, like when someone says he or she is going to talk about four topics and talks about only three. In general, it allows us to compartmentalize many aspects of our lives so we can do what is necessary to accomplish our objectives.

ACTIVITY

Look around you again and find some items to organize in the room. File some papers. Sort some mail. Organize something or try to understand the system of logic someone else used!

Introverted Thinking (T$_i$)

> Think about those apples again. What kinds of things are apples anyway? List the categories that apples fall into.

Introverted Thinking (coded as T$_i$) involves a process of directing your attention inward to the categories and principles that can help you figure out what is going on or to classify something. Analyzing, checking consistency, defining, and matching—all involve introverted Thinking. If you were to look outside at an apple tree, you might notice that the leaves are falling off early. Using the process of introverted Thinking, you would analyze the situation and try to figure out what is wrong with the tree. You might use the principles of good gardening, or you might reference the scientific principles of plant disease. The cognitive process of introverted Thinking involves having internal frameworks, models, or blueprints to check things against and techniques and approaches for fixing them. The more clear, accurate, and internally consistent the model, the better this process works. These principles and frameworks operate in and can be applied to many challenges. Being clear about the principles and the models helps us figure out solutions and answers to any situation for a better approach.

Introverted Thinking often involves finding just the right word to clearly express an idea concisely, crisply, and to the point. Using introverted Thinking is

NOTE
Thinking as a cognitive process does not mean the same thing as the usual meaning of thinking. Neither does it imply intelligence. In this model, there are many kinds of intelligence.

The Philosophy of Life That Engages Introverted Thinking:

Everything can be explained and understood in terms of how it works.

Examples of introverted Thinking:

- On the way home, Lenore went into the pet store with her checklist. She looked at a cocker spaniel and a standard poodle and found out how big each one grew and if it barked a lot. She decided the standard poodle didn't meet her criteria but wasn't sure about the cocker—she thought maybe she should consider a dachshund.
- David analyzed the successful methods used by experts, then described what techniques to use to be successful.
- Right away, May started analyzing the earthquake as to intensity, kind, and probable fault location. She had many models in her head about earthquakes and was already fitting the data into them.

like having an internal sense of the essential qualities of something, noticing the fine distinctions that make it what it is and then naming it. It also involves an internal reasoning process of deriving subcategories of classes and sub-principles of general principles. These can then be used in problem solving, analysis, and refining of a product or an idea.

This process is evidenced in behaviors like taking things or ideas apart to figure out how they work. The analysis involves looking at different sides of an issue and seeing where there is inconsistency. In so doing, there is a search for a "leverage point" that will fix problems with the least amount of effort or damage to the system.

ACTIVITY

Look around you again and name some of the objects in the room. What classes or categories are they members of? As you classify them, check against the objective categories you hold mentally.

Which fits you? As you read and reflect on the two ways of using the cognitive process of Thinking, does one feel easier and more comfortable? When making principle-based evaluations, which mode are you more likely to use or to trust more?

● **extraverted Thinking or introverted Thinking** ●

The Cognitive Processes of Feeling

Feeling is a process of making evaluations based on what is important, where personal, interpersonal, or universal values serve as guideposts. Using the cognitive process of Feeling, situations and information are assessed subjectively. The impact on people, circumstances, appropriateness, harmony, likes, and dislikes are all considered in making Feeling judgments. Weighing different values, considering ethical and moral issues, attending to personal and relationship goals, and having a belief in something all involve this process.

Extraverted Feeling (F$_e$)

Think about those apples again. As you notice the apples, ask yourself which of your friends or family members like apples. Do they like raw apples better than they like apple pie?

Extraverted Feeling (coded as F$_e$) involves a process of arranging the external world according to interpersonal importance. We use this process when we consider what is important to others and what is appropriate to a situation. Again, if you imagine looking out the window at an apple tree, you might think about removing the apple tree because of the mess the apples make on the ground, but then you remember that your family really likes having that old apple tree around. So you decide not to remove it. Besides, you might think, Aunt Mary really likes apple pie made with those apples. You make a mental note to bake an apple pie for her. In deciding what to do with

The Philosophy of Life That Engages Extraverted Feeling:

Everything can be considered in terms of how it affects others.

Examples of extraverted Feeling:

- Lenore thought about what kind of dog her sister would want. She knew her sister would be disappointed if they couldn't get a standard poodle, so she decided to not even mention that the one in the pet store was still there.
- In doing the budget, George decided to get input from everyone, not just the managers. Knowing what is important to everyone would make the whole team work better.
- May was concerned that her mother was feeling even more vulnerable after the earthquake, so she made a special effort to see her more often.

the tree, the likes and dislikes of others are considered and adjusted to. The extraverted Feeling process is used in relation to particular people and situations and so has a more here-and-now quality than a universal, future, or past quality. When particular people are out of our presence or awareness, we can then adjust to new people or situations. This process helps us "grease the wheels" of social interaction.

Often, the process of extraverted Feeling seems to involve a desire to connect with (or disconnect from) others and is often evidenced by expressions of warmth (or displeasure) and self-disclosure. The "social graces" such as being polite, being nice, being friendly, being considerate, and being appropriate often revolve around the process of extraverted Feeling. Associated behaviors might include remembering birthdays, finding just the right card for a person and selecting a gift based on what a person likes. Keeping in touch, laughing at jokes when others laugh, and trying to get people to act kindly to each other also involve extraverted Feeling. Using this process, we respond according to expressed or even unexpressed wants and needs of others. We may ask people what they want or need or self-disclose to prompt them to talk more about themselves. This often sparks conversation and lets us know more about them so we can better adjust our behavior to them.

ACTIVITY

Ask yourself whose birthdays are coming soon. What do you think of to get for them? What do they like? Would they like a surprise party or a singing telegram? Should you get them a sentimental card or a humorous card? What would they most enjoy?

Introverted Feeling (F$_i$)

The Philosophy of Life That Engages Introverted Feeling:

Everything can be in harmony or congruence.

Examples of introverted Feeling:

- Lenore's sister came home with a standard poodle. When Lenore asked her why, her sister said, "We've always wanted a standard poodle like we used to have. This one was so cute and was going to be sent to the pound, so I just had to bring it home."
- Martha kept pointing out that what was really important was the success of the project for the company as well as for the individual.
- After the earthquake, John detected that some of his students were acting like "business as usual," even though he believed they were deeply affected by the trauma of the earthquake.

> Think about those apples again. Do you like apples? Apple pie? Or consider whether apples are really important or worthwhile.

Introverted Feeling (coded as F$_i$) involves a process of deciding and evaluating according to importance. Importance can be decided on the basis of personal values such as "I want," "I don't want," "I like," or "I don't like," or universal values such as "This is good" or "This is bad." In deciding what to do with an apple tree outside your window, you might reflect on how much you really like that tree and the apples it yields. You might even consider the importance of having a fruit tree for the children to learn from. When you use this process, you may reference how you feel to give yourself the information you need to make a decision. The process of introverted Feeling involves checking a proposed action against a personal or universal value to see if it is congruent. Being in touch with our values and beliefs allows us to respond congruently to any situation no matter what happens. Loyalty and commitment can stem from decisions made using this process since these values are not bound to a particular time, context, or situation.

It is often hard to put words to the values used to make introverted Feeling judgments since they are often associated with images and feeling-tones more than words. As a cognitive process, it often serves as a filter for information that matches what is valued and wanted. We engage in the process of introverted Feeling when a value is compromised and we think, "sometimes, some things just have to be said." On the other hand, most of the time this process works "in private" and is seldom expressed directly. Actions often speak louder than words.

This process helps us know when people are being fake or insincere or if they are basically good. It is like having an internal sense of the "essence" of a person or a project, and reading another person or action or project with fine distinctions among feeling-tones. When the other person's values and beliefs are congruent with our own, we are inclined to feel kinship with them and want to connect with them.

ACTIVITY — As you look around your environment, what do you see that you like or dislike? What is most important for you or your family, friends, or coworkers to do next?

Which fits you? As you read and reflect on the two ways of using the cognitive process of Feeling, does one feel easier and more comfortable? When making value-based evaluations, which mode are you more likely to use or trust more?

● **extraverted Feeling or introverted Feeling** ●

> **NOTE**
> Feeling, as a cognitive process, is not the same thing as becoming emotional or having feelings. However, emotion and feelings provide good information to help clarify values and importance. Also, it is not just "touchy feely," but rather plays a valuable role in making decisions that people stick to.

Preferred Processes

Preferences for Certain Processes

Did you notice that some of the activities were easier to do than others? What made them easier? Sometimes this comes from practice, and sometimes it is a natural preference.

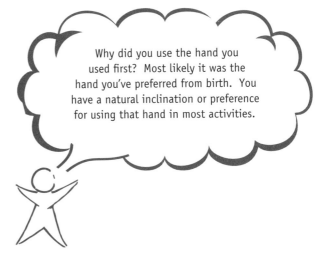

Why did you use the hand you used first? Most likely it was the hand you've preferred from birth. You have a natural inclination or preference for using that hand in most activities.

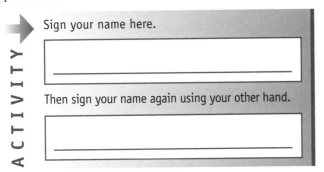

A C T I V I T Y

Sign your name here.

Then sign your name again using your other hand.

Just like with handedness, we seem to have innate preferences for *one* of the four perceptive processes (S_e, S_i, N_e, or N_i) and *one* of the four judging processes (T_e, T_i, F_e, or F_i).

However, just as you were able to use your non preferred hand, you can and do engage all eight cognitive processes at different times and at different levels of proficiency.

Here is the chart from page 14 with the names of Jung's cognitive processes.

The Cognitive Processes and Learning	Name of Cognitive Process
INFORMATION-ACCESSING PROCESSES	
Experiencing and noticing the physical world, scanning for visible reactions and relevant data What is really happening? What are the facts of the situation? What can I do with this now?	extraverted Sensing (S_e)
Recalling past experiences, remembering detailed data and what it is linked to What have I already learned that I can build on? What resources and materials are available? What practical use does this have?	introverted Sensing (S_i)
Inferring relationships, noticing threads of meaning, and scanning for what could be What inferences can I make? What meanings am I perceiving? What hypotheses can I generate?	extraverted iNtuiting (N_e)
Foreseeing implications, conceptualizing, and having images of the future or profound meaning What are the implications for the future? What are the concepts? What is the greater purpose?	introverted iNtuiting (N_i)
EVALUATING PROCESSES	
Organizing, segmenting, sorting, and applying logic and criteria How can I structure and organize my learning? What is the sequence and arrangement of what I am learning? What is the logic behind what I am learning?	extraverted Thinking (T_e)
Analyzing, categorizing, and figuring out how something works What principles do I need to learn? What models can I fit the learning into? What techniques or approaches can I apply?	introverted Thinking (T_i)
Considering others and responding to them Who can I connect with, or relate to in order to learn better? Who can I help with this learning? How can I use this to improve my relationships?	extraverted Feeling (F_e)
Evaluating importance and maintaining congruence What is really important here? What is of value to me, and what do I want out of this? Who is good to learn from?	introverted Feeling (F_i)

Preference ≠ Skill

Having a preference does not necessarily result in skill development. Practice is what develops skill. Preference is likely to determine the ease with which we develop a skill and how attractive we find the exercise of the skill.

"The present system of public education succeeds with particular types but fails to bring many students to a satisfactory state of maturity."
—Isabel Briggs Myers*

If the environment allows, we will usually engage in (practice) the processes that come naturally to us and thus get good at doing them. However, we can develop skill in the other cognitive processes, even if they are not our preferences. School experiences provide us with good examples of this. When we go to school, we learn to organize the external world according to various systems of logic—alphabetizing, sequencing, outlining, and so on. This gives us practice in simple extraverted Thinking. We gain experience in introverted Thinking as we are taught categories and principles early on, and then later how to critique according to those categories and principles.

As early as preschool and kindergarten, we are taught to be considerate of our classmates and what is appropriate behavior in a situation (extraverted Feeling). Introverted feeling comes into play when we are given moral dilemmas to solve. (One might comment that in most schools, not much curriculum time is devoted to teaching how to develop skill in extraverted Feeling or introverted Feeling. That is mostly left to the family, community, and church.)

Learning Style	Preferred Processes
Guide	introverted iNtuiting and extraverted Feeling
Mediator	extraverted iNtuiting and introverted Feeling
Coordinator	introverted iNtuiting and extraverted Thinking
Engineer	extraverted iNtuiting and introverted Thinking
Monitor	introverted Sensing and extraverted Thinking
Conservator	introverted Sensing and extraverted Feeling
Expeditor	extraverted Sensing and introverted Thinking
Improvisor	extraverted Sensing and introverted Feeling

Review the selections you made on the previous pages. Which learning patterns reflect the processes you selected as more comfortable for you? Are they the same learning patterns you selected as reflecting your natural learning style? We'll come back to these questions later. For now, let's look at some differences in these patterns.

Now go back and look at your selected favorite and least favorite learning pattern descriptions on pages 12–13. Apply what you've learned and identify the processes used in those patterns. The two main processes used in each one are listed above in the table to the right.

On the following two pages you'll find variations in the eight patterns. Use your self-selected learning patterns from page 14 to see if you can find one or two of them that feel right for you. Put a check mark on the ones that fit you.

---

*Isabel Briggs Myers with Peter B. Myers, *Gifts Differing: Understanding Personality Type* (Palo Alto, CA: Davies-Black Publishing, 1995), 167.

The Guide Learning Style

Foreseer Developer

When learning is focused on personal growth and sustaining a vision, that is most rewarding. Using my talent for foreseeing, I like learning that helps others explore issues and bridge differences, as well as learning that connects people. I really want my learning to help me live my idealistic life, so it must include practical problem-solving to be really valuable. I honor the gifts of others, and love to learn what I can do to help them develop those gifts. If what I am learning helps me take a creative approach to life and live with a greater sense of purpose, so much the better.

Envisioner Mentor

My most rewarding learning experiences include opportunities to communicate and share values, and to help myself and others succeed in relationships. I seek learning opportunities where I can grow, and that help me heed the call to a life work or mission. I enjoy the creative process and using my intuitive intellect to find ways to reconcile the past and the future. All of these help me see the potential in others, and I like learning more about how to help them achieve their potential. I love to learn how to help realize dreams—my own and others'.

The Mediator Learning Style

Harmonizer Clarifier

I learn best when I can just go with the flow. I like uncovering mysteries and exploring moral questions. I relate through stories and metaphors that help me balance the many opposing forces of life. I have a way of knowing what is behind what is said, so sometimes that is what grabs my attention. I use my talent for facilitative listening to really learn, especially about myself and others. Learning that helps me get reacquainted with myself is the most rewarding. I have a way of knowing what is believable and will judge my learning experience by that.

Discoverer Advocate

My most meaningful learning is inspiring and helps me facilitate others. If my learning provides me with what I need to authentically live with myself, then I can learn anything. I need an opportunity to respond to insights in the creative process. Recognizing happiness, living out stories, and finding the magical situation all motivate me to learn. I love exploring perceptions, seeing what's not being said, and voicing unspoken meanings. Sometimes this talent of mine can interfere with my learning if too much is going on beneath the surface, getting in the way of relationships.

The Coordinator Learning Style

Conceptualizer Director

Learning is all about progress. I have an intense drive for self-mastery. I want my learning to help me build a vision with very long-range strategizing. I seek learning experiences that help me maximize achievements toward goals and be on the leading edge. I like learning experiences that use my natural way of systems thinking, where I can maintain my independence and find a way to reconceptualize. Sometimes this takes some reflection time, but other times it's going on in the background during the learning experience as I see the reasons behind things.

Strategist Mobilizer

Learning helps me marshal resources toward progress. I often find myself being a leader, and I want to learn to better maximize talents—my own as well as the talents of others. I approach my learning as I do everything else—by forging partnerships. My goal is to become more competent, and I view most of life as a learning experience. This helps me balance peace and conflict. I use my talent for coordinating to apply my learning to multiple projects, even during the learning experience itself. I really enjoy intuitive explorations. I often have a kind of predictive creativity that helps me know what is important to learn.

The Engineer Learning Style

Designer Theorizer

Learning, like life, is about becoming an expert, knowing all there is to know about something. I like learning that helps me see new patterns and elegant connections, cross the artificial boundaries of thought, and activate the imagination. I even like to reflect on the process of thinking itself. Intellectual discussions where we can clarify and define concepts help me learn. Sometimes in those discussions, I detach from the situation to analyze. Then I come back with a discovery that helps make things clearer.

Explorer Inventor

Learning is about being inventive, seeing patterns and connections that lead to prototypes, and getting projects launched. I'm a lifelong learner, and I want to strategically formulate my success so I can learn from anything, anytime, anywhere. I really enjoy the creative process, and my best learning occurs when I get to share my insights about life's possibilities with others as they occur. The drama of give-and-take in a lively debate really helps me learn. I try to be diplomatic, but sometimes making a point in a discussion takes priority.

The Monitor Learning Style

Planner Inspector

I take responsibility for my learning and am loyal to my role as a student. I want to be prepared and will plan how I'm going to learn something. I want to get the work done first, then I can relax. If the learning experience turns out to be harder than I thought, I will do the right thing and overcome the adversity of the experience by working hard at it. I like cultivating good qualities and will bear the burden of difficult learning experiences to accomplish that. It helps if the learning is well organized, where nothing is missing or out of sequence.

Implementor Supervisor

I really like to educate myself about things and I seek out the necessary learning experiences. Learning helps me bring order to chaotic situations, be well-balanced, and formulate the steps to success. I approach learning with my usual industrious, work-hard attitude, but I do like to balance work with play. I have a philosophy of life and I learn best when I can connect my wealth of life experiences to what I am learning. I apply my own high standards economy and quality to my learning experiences, just like I do in the rest of my life.

The Conservator Learning Style

Protector Supporter

In my learning I like having an opportunity to notice what's needed and what's valuable, and to know the ins and outs of things. I enjoy traditions and knowing what to expect. I want the purpose of my learning to be to help me work to protect the future. Careful and supportive organization, and an opportunity to listen and remember help me learn. I get exasperated when people ignore rules and don't get along. Being nice and agreeable is the best thing an instructor can do for me besides help me feel a sense of accomplishment.

Facilitator Caretaker

I love learning anything that will help people accept and help each other. That kind of learning just comes naturally. I want to be in a learning environment where I can hear people, and where concerns are voiced and needs accommodated. I truly admire the success of others, and hearing about those successes helps me learn. I think managing people is the most important part of the learning experience. If it's done well, I can learn. If not, then I'll try to provide others with what they need and keep the situation pleasant. I learn better if the instructor maintains a sense of continuity and remembers what's important.

The Expeditor Learning Style

Analyzer Operator

To get me excited about learning, let me actively solve problems. I like to observe how things work and to truly understand a situation. Sometimes that means taking things apart and making discoveries. I like learning how to use tools, but let me be independent and learn by doing rather than just reading. I want to find all the angles, so let me question and challenge. If you give me the framework or the model, I'll find the best approach. I enjoy getting hunches about how things work and applying the models to solve problems.

Promoter Executor

I learn best when I have the freedom to tactically prioritize what to learn and when to learn it. I like taking charge of a situation and that includes my learning. Sometimes I'll even end up acting as a consultant to help the teacher, if I'm given half a chance to respectfully show what I know. I remember an incredible amount of information if I know I'll have an opportunity to use it and see how it fits into what I have to do. I want to have a measure of how well I've performed.

The Improvisor Learning Style

Composer Producer

I'm most interested in sticking with what's important and not just learning because it's required. I like learning that helps me take advantage of opportunities. It's fun to be able to pull things together and use my learning for creative problem-solving. I enjoy building relationships, and having a relationship with my fellow learners as well as the teacher is important. I do have my own personal style and need to be true to myself. Sometimes I get into playing against the expectations of others just for the learning and the experience that comes from it.

Motivator Presenter

I love to learn, especially about people. I want to be engaged in my learning through stimulating action and personal involvement. Since I love opening up people to possibilities, I want an opportunity to share the possibilities I see when I see them. It also helps if there is a little drama, flair, and style to the teaching. I need to feel that the teacher genuinely cares. I need to have enough of a grasp of a subject so I can make sense of it. Then I'll learn all I need as long as I can see what I am going to do with what I learn.

Patterns of Processes

The cognitive processes always occur in the context of a pattern, never in isolation.

In this pattern, each process seems to play a certain kind of role. For example, in your preferred learning pattern, two processes are used primarily. When we look at more differences, we can see that one process takes a leading role and the other takes a supporting role.*

List the name of your best-fit learning pattern: (see pgs.28–29)

Here are the leading and supporting role processes for each pattern

Foreseer Developer N_i F_e	Harmonizer Clarifier F_i N_e	Planner Inspector S_i T_e	Protector Supporter S_i F_e
Envisioner Mentor F_e N_i	Discoverer Advocate N_e F_i	Implementor Supervisor T_e S_i	Facilitator Caretaker F_e S_i
Conceptualizer Director N_i T_e	Designer Theorizer T_i N_e	Analyzer Operator T_i S_e	Composer Producer F_i S_e
Strategist Mobilizer T_e N_i	Explorer Inventor N_e T_i	Promoter Executor S_e T_i	Motivator Presenter S_e F_i

---

There are 16 personality types. **
Each "type" represents a unique *predictable* pattern of how the eight processes are used in everyday life.

In truth, we have access to all eight cognitive processes—the other six are often in the background, playing other kinds of roles. Each has a positive and a negative way of expressing itself. Each bears a different energy cost when we use them.

Development of the Primary Processes***

The primary processes are those used in the first four roles. These processes tend to emerge and develop at different times in our lives. During these times we are drawn to activities that use these processes. Then, learning the content and the skills that engage these processes is often nearly effortless. We find our interest is drawn to them and our interest is pulled away from things we were drawn to before.

The Leading Role

The process that plays the leading role is the one that usually develops early in childhood. We tend to engage in this process first, trusting it to solve our problems and help us be successful. Being the most trusted and most used, it usually has an adult, mature quality to it. While we are likely to engage in it rather automatically and effortlessly, we have much more conscious control over it. The energy cost for using it is very low. Much like in the movies, the leading role has a heroic quality as it can get us out of difficult situations. However, we can sometimes "turn up the volume" on this process and become overbearing and domineering. Then it takes on a negative dominating quality.

The Supporting Role

The supporting role is how we are helpful to others as well as supportive of ourselves. Once we have developed some facility with our leading role process, we are likely to engage a different process in supporting role behavior. In its most positive form, it can be quite like a nurturing parent. In its more negative aspect, it can be overprotective and stunting rather than helpful. When the leading role process is an extraverted one, the supporting role process is introverted. When the leading role process is an introverted one, the supporting role process is extraverted and may be quite active and visible as it provides a way of dealing with the outer world.

The Relief Role

The relief role gives us a way to energize and recharge ourselves. It serves as backup to the supporting role and often works in tandem with it. When we are younger, we might not engage in the process that plays this role very much unless our life circumstances require it or make

---

* The roles of the cognitive processes are an expansion of the work of John Beebe, a Jungian analyst.

**For more information on the sixteen personality types, see Appendix D: References.

*** In the Jungian model, the first four roles are referred to as Dominant, Auxiliary, Tertiary and Inferior. We use Leading, Supporting, Relief and Idealistic as descriptive terms for ease of understanding.

it hard to use the supporting role process. Usually, in young adulthood we are drawn to activities that draw upon this process. The relief role often is how we express our creativity. It is how we are playful and childlike. In its most negative expression, this is how we become childish. Then it has an unsettling quality, and we can use it to distract ourselves and others, getting us off target.

The Aspirational Role

The aspirational role usually doesn't develop until around midlife. We often experience it first in its negative aspect of projecting of our "shoulds," fears, and negativities onto others. The qualities of these fears reflect the process that plays this role, so we are likely to look immature when we engage in the process that plays this role. There is often a fairly high energy cost for using it—even when we acquire the skill to do so. As we learn to trust it and develop it, the idealistic role process provides a bridge to balance in our lives. Often our sense of purpose, inspiration, and ideals have the qualities of the process that plays this role.

The Shadow Processes

The other four cognitive processes operate more on the boundaries of our awareness. It is as if they are in the shadows and only come forward under certain circumstances. They are like the "spear bearer" in the theater—an unknown, coming on to the stage, bearing a "spear." We usually experience them in a negative way, yet when we are open to them, they can be quite positive.

The Opposing Role

The opposing role is often how we get stubborn and argumentative—refusing to "play" and join in whatever is going on at the time. It might be easy for us to develop skill in the process that plays this role, but we are likely to be more narrow in our application of this skill, and it will likely take more energy to use it extensively. In its positive aspect, it provides a shadow or depth to our leading role process, backing it up and enabling us to be more persistent in pursuit of our goals.

The Critical Parent Role

The critical parent role is how we find weak spots and can immobilize and demoralize ourselves and others. The process that plays this role is often sporadic in its appearance and emerges more often under stressful conditions when something important is at risk. When it does appear, it can go on and on. To access its positive side of discovery, we must learn to appreciate its presence and be open to it. Then it has an almost magical quality and can provide a profound sense of knowing and wisdom.

The Deceiving Role

The deceiving role fools us into thinking something is important to do or pay attention to. The process that fills this role is often not trusted or seen as worthy of attention, for when we do pay attention to it, we may make mistakes in perception or in making decisions. It can paralyze and double bind us. Yet this role can have a positive side as it provides comic relief. Then we can laugh at ourselves. It can be refreshing and join with the relief role as we recharge ourselves through play.

The Devilish Role

The devilish role can be quite negative. Using the process that plays this role, we might become destructive of ourselves or others. Actions (or inactions) taken when we engage the process that plays this role are often regretted later. Usually, we are unaware of how to use the process that fills this role and it just erupts and imposes itself rather unconsciously. Yet when we are open to the process that plays the devilish role, it becomes transformative. It gives us the impetus to create something new—to make lemonade out of lemons, rather than lament their sourness.

Keep in mind that we are not always aware of how some of the processes play out in our own personalities. Therefore, we are likely to not recognize them in ourselves or the value they can bring to an endeavor.

	Characteristics Known to Self	Characteristics Unknown to Self
Competence (proficiency/ skill)	Cognitive processes we have just developed skill in or that stand out when we engage them since they are not as automatic for us.	We are often blind to our habitual ways of processing. These most likely represent inborn tendencies and how we have operated from a very early age.
Incompetence (inadequacy/ inexperience)	Cognitive processes we may have just become aware of and that we try to use, but don't feel skilled in yet.	Our blind spots. The cognitive processes that we don't even know exist, so we are unaware of our incompetence and more importantly, the value they can contribute.

We are more likely to identify and claim those processes we are aware of, rather than those we are unaware of. If we are competent in using the process, yet unaware of it, we will take it for granted. If we are incompetent and unaware, we are likely to project the negative aspects of this process onto others and even deny that it can have any value anywhere.

Here are the roles of the processes that go with the sixteen learning patterns. They are listed from top to bottom in a hierarchy. This hierarchy suggests how much the energy cost would be for engaging the process that plays that role. The first two are usually readily available to us and have a very low energy cost. The next two often become more available to us as we develop over time. Still, they may bear a higher energy cost, especially the aspirational one. These are the cognitive processes we are likely to be drawn to develop in our adulthood. The last four are often experienced negatively more often than positively, but we can learn to be more receptive to a positive expression of them. Based on the learning pattern(s) that fit you best, use these charts to complete the activities on the following pages.

Your Best-Fit Learning Pattern:

The Roles and Processes of the Sixteen Personality Types

	Guide		Mediator		Monitor		Conservator	
	Envisioner Mentor ENFJ	Foreseer Developer INFJ	Discoverer Advocate ENFP	Harmonizer Clarifier INFP	Implementor Supervisor ESTJ	Planner Inspector ISTJ	Facilitator Caretaker ESFJ	Protector Supporter ISFJ
1st + Leading − Dominating	F_e	N_i	N_e	F_i	T_e	S_i	F_e	S_i
2nd + Supporting − Overprotective	N_i	F_e	F_i	N_e	S_i	T_e	S_i	F_e
3rd + Relief − Unsettling	S_e	T_i	T_e	S_i	N_e	F_i	N_e	T_i
4th + Aspirational − Projective	T_i	S_e	S_i	T_e	F_i	N_e	T_i	N_e
5th − Opposing + Backup	F_i	N_e	N_i	F_e	T_i	S_e	F_i	S_e
6th − Critical + Discovery	N_e	F_i	F_e	N_i	S_e	T_i	S_e	F_i
7th − Deceiving + Comedic	S_i	T_e	T_i	S_e	N_i	F_e	N_i	T_e
8th − Devilish + Transformative	T_e	S_i	S_e	T_i	F_e	N_i	T_e	N_i

	Coordinator		Engineer		Expeditor		Improvisor	
	Strategist Mobilizer ENTJ	Conceptualizer Director INTJ	Explorer Inventor ENTP	Designer Theorizer INTP	Promoter Executor ESTP	Analyzer Operator ISTP	Motivator Presenter ESFP	Composer Producer ISFP
1st + Leading − Dominating	T_e	N_i	N_e	T_i	S_e	T_i	S_e	F_i
2nd + Supporting − Overprotective	N_i	T_e	T_i	N_e	T_i	S_e	F_i	S_e
3rd + Relief − Unsettling	S_e	F_i	F_e	S_i	F_e	N_i	T_e	N_i
4th + Aspirational − Projective	F_i	S_e	S_i	F_e	N_i	F_e	N_i	T_e
5th − Opposing + Backup	T_i	N_e	N_i	T_e	S_i	T_e	S_i	F_e
6th − Critical + Discovery	N_e	T_i	T_e	N_i	T_e	S_i	F_e	S_i
7th − Deceiving + Comedic	S_i	F_e	F_i	S_e	F_i	N_e	T_i	N_e
8th − Devilish + Transformative	F_e	S_i	S_e	F_i	N_e	F_i	N_e	T_i

Your Patterns

Let's integrate your experience exploring the cognitive processes with your experience of applying them to your learning pattern. First, review the descriptions of the cognitive processes (pages 18–25) and rate each process along the dimensions that follow.

Energy Cost

When (or if) you engage in the activities associated with this process, how energizing is it? If you find it exhausting, there is a high energy cost. If it is energizing, there is a low energy cost.

Availability

If you engage in the process so automatically you don't even notice it, but others would say you do it, then consider it on the automatic side. If you don't even know how to do the process even if you wanted to, rate it a 1. In-between means you can get it started if the situation is right or if you are mirroring someone else.

Confidence

Confidence means you can trust the process to work for you most of the time. When you use that process, you tend to feel self-confident.

Importance to You

This means you find it valuable enough to you personally to set a high priority on those activities. "Worthless" means you tend to put off activities of this nature even if you think they are important to a project or important in general.

Development

To answer on this rating scale, ask yourself if you've always used the process. You may remember a specific time when you learned it or your interest in activities shifted toward this process.

Try to think in terms of how you are naturally and have been over your lifetime, rather than processes you recently learned or developed.

Integrating Your Experiences

☹ ☺ 1 2 3 4 5	S_e Experiencing	S_i Recalling	N_e Inferring	N_i Foreseeing	T_e Organizing	T_i Analyzing	F_e Considering Others	F_i Evaluating Importance
energy cost high low 1 2 3 4 5								
availability jump-start automatic 1 2 3 4 5								
confidence hesitant confident 1 2 3 4 5								
importance to you worthless valued 1 2 3 4 5								
development learned natural 1 2 3 4 5								
TOTAL POINTS	S_e	S_i	N_e	N_i	T_e	T_i	F_e	F_i

Now rank the processes according to the total ratings you gave them. Also list the hierarchy suggested by your best-fit learning pattern. If you get feedback from others, list that. If you have completed a personality instrument like the MBTI, list the ranking from that. (The role hierarchy pattern for the MBTI codes is presented on page 32.)

Which processes play which role in your personality?

Roles of the Processes	Self-Ranking (from page 14)	Your Learning Pattern Hierarchy (from page 32)	Feedback from Others	Feedback from Instruments (like MBTI)	Your Best-Fit Pattern of Processes
+ Leading 1st - Dominating					
+ Supporting 2nd - Overprotective					
+ Relief 3rd - Unsettling					
+ Aspirational 4th - Projective					
- Opposing 5th + Backup					
- Critical 6th + Discovery					
- Deceiving 7th + Comedic					
- Devilish 8th + Transformative					

Do the rankings match? Is one a more developed pattern? Is one a more contextual pattern? Which column represents your true self? If some of the patterns are different, don't be concerned. It may reflect a newly acquired skill or the actual development of a process in yourself. It may be a sign you need to do even more exploring to know yourself better.*

---

* If you feel you still need to find your best-fit type, Appendix A may be helpful, or you may want to get professional facilitation for your self-discovery process.

Take Charge of Your Learning

We are born to learn. Learning is how we grow and develop. It is how we adjust and adapt to an ever-changing and demanding world.

When we look at learning, we need to examine three factors:

1. What—the content or skill to be learned
2. How—the learning context
3. Who—the learning style of the learner

When all of these factors are congruent, the result is effective, efficient learning. When they are not congruent, at best we have a high energy cost, and at worst we have no learning.

To take charge of your own learning, capitalize on lessons from the past to plan for the future. Think about the cognitive processes we just explored, as well as your descriptions of your best and worst learning experiences. Answer the following questions and then think of your preferred learning pattern to anticipate what will make your next learning experience better.

"Learning is not a task or a problem; it is a way to be in the world."
—Sidney Jourard*

Your Learning Experiences	Best Learning Experience(s)	Worst Learning Experience(s)
• What was being taught or learned? • What cognitive processes seemed to be activated by the content or task?		
• What was the context of the learning—instructional techniques being used, atmosphere, environment, purpose, behaviors and mannerisms of the instructor (if there was one), behaviors of others, and so on? • What cognitive processes seemed to be encouraged by the environment?		
• How well did your preferences in your learning style match or mismatch the content and the context? • What cognitive processes did you have to stretch to use? • When the learning involved processes other than your preferred ones (leading or supporting roles), what helped you learn in spite of everything?		

What learning conditions do you need to arrange for yourself in your future learning experiences?

REMEMBER

If the content or the context is going to require you to operate from other than your leading or supporting role processes, be patient with yourself. Allow extra time. Be extra forgiving. Get a coach. Ask for what you need. Often an instructor can provide it, if you only ask for it.

---

*As quoted in Malcolm Knowles, *The Adult Learner: A Neglected Species* (Houston, Texas: Gulf Publishing Company, 1990), 91.

Problem Solving and Communication

Problem Solving

Most of the time, our daily lives go along on autopilot. However, when things are not going well, we may stop and try to apply a formal problem-solving or decision-making process.

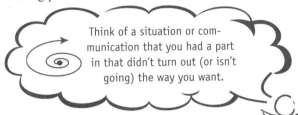

Think of a situation or communication that you had a part in that didn't turn out (or isn't going) the way you want.

Our type code can give us clues as to which processes we are most likely to use in any given situation, but we do have the possibility of using any of them and most likely do use more than two. The problem comes when we overuse some and under use others and get stuck. As we get more and more stressed, we are likely to do just that.

A Personal Example

On the last day of a stressful five-and-a-half-day workshop with a group of army officers, I drove into the parking lot. I went up to the door of the building and it was locked. I went back to the car and waited a long time and then finally went to investigate around the corner. I then noticed that everyone had parked on the other side of the building. I realized that it was Saturday, so the building probably was not all opened up. Frustrated and angry, I went up the stairs, stormed into the meeting room, and complained, "It would have been nice if someone had told me the usual doors were locked!" The poor participants were upset at my being late and anxious about the exam they had to take. My outburst didn't set a good tone for the end of the workshop.

> *"No problem can be solved from the same consciousness that created it."*
> **—Albert Einstein**

Analyzing the problem later, I realized I had "turned up the volume" on my preferred cognitive processes and ignored my less-preferred processes, or engaged them only in desperation and very poorly at that.

My type pattern reflects how much and how well I used the cognitive processes in approaching the problem:

Roles of the Processes	Designer Theorizer INTP
+ Leading - Dominating	T_i—introverted Thinking
+ Supporting - Overprotective	N_e—extraverted iNtuiting
+ Relief - Unsettling	S_i—introverted Sensing
+ Aspirational - Projective	F_e—extraverted Feeling
- Opposing + Backup	T_e—extraverted Thinking
- Critical + Discovery	N_i—introverted iNtuiting
- Deceiving + Comedic	S_e—extraverted Sensing
- Devilish + Transformative	F_i—introverted Feeling

Knowing our own pattern can help us see our blind spots and help us find ways we can get out of the "consciousness" that helped produce a problem.

As I drove up to the building, extraverted Sensing information was available to me, but I ignored it. I was so involved in analyzing my week using introverted Thinking and seeking meaning and hypothesizing about it using extraverted iNtuiting that I didn't notice all the cars in front of the building. I went around the building to my usual parking place, using introverted Sensing in the background and rather unconsciously. Then, instead of gathering new data via extraverted Sensing, I went back to the car and back to using my preferred processes! When I finally got a sense of something not being right, I switched to a very inferior extraverted Feeling process and projected blame onto my "victims." I had totally omitted any consideration of what was appropriate or what that group of usually-prompt people was like. But the story does have a decent ending. It was a workshop qualifying participants to purchase the MBTI, and we were later able to analyze the experience and understand what had happened. Now when I get in situations that aren't going the way I want, I am more likely to ask myself what process I am stuck in or what process I am ignoring.

The Eight Cognitive Processes in Problem Solving and Decision Making

	Names of The Roles This Process Plays in My Pattern (Both Positive and Negative)
INFORMATION-ACCESSING PROCESSES (Perception)	
S_e—**Experiencing** and noticing the physical world, scanning for visible reactions and relevant data. What is really happening? What are the facts of the situation? What is changing in this situation? What action can I take now?	
S_i—**Recalling** past experiences, remembering detailed data and what it is linked to. What do I already know that I can build on? What usually happens in this kind of situation? How does what is happening here remind me of some problem I have previously solved?	
N_e—**Inferring** relationships, noticing threads of meaning, and scanning for what could be. What inferences do I need to make? What meanings do I need to perceive? What hypotheses can I generate?	
N_i—**Foreseeing** implications, conceptualizing, and having images of the future or profound meaning. What are the implications for the future? What do I need to conceptualize? How will so-and-so respond if I do such-and-such?	
EVALUATING PROCESSES (Judgment)	
T_e—**Organizing**, segmenting, sorting, and applying logic and criteria. How is this situation structured and organized? What logic and criteria apply? How can I break something down into its component parts and organize, arrange, and coordinate it for more efficient results?	
T_i—**Analyzing**, categorizing, and figuring out how something works. What principles do I need to apply? What models are operating here? What techniques or approaches can I apply?	
F_e—**Considering others** and responding to them. Whose needs do I need to consider? What is important to these people? What is appropriate in this situation? What is good for the group?	
F_i—**Evaluating importance** and maintaining congruence. What is really important here? What is of value to me and to the purpose? What values are at stake? What values have been violated?	

Philosophies of Life That Engage the Perceiving Processes

S_e—There is always more to be experienced, and opportunities don't last.

N_e—There are always other perspectives and new meanings to discover.

S_i—There is always a comparison to be made, and if it is familiar it is to be trusted.

N_i—There is always a future to realize and a significance to be revealed.

Philosophies of Life That Engage the Judging Processes

T_e—Everything can be logical, structured, and organized.

F_e—Everything can be considered in terms of how it affects others.

T_i—Everything can be explained and understood in terms of how it works.

F_i—Everything can be in harmony or congruence.

Consider which processes play the leading and supporting roles in your pattern. Pick the philosophies of life that engage these two processes and you will have a probable description of your habitual problem-solving style.

As you review the essential qualities of the cognitive processes on the following pages, think of how each process plays out in your life. Then, answer the reflection questions to apply your understanding to the problem situation you thought of on page 36.

Essential Characteristics of the Perceiving Processes

Extraverted Sensing S_e

—**Experiencing**
—**Doing**
—**Observing and Responding**
—**Adapting and Varying**
—*Present*

- Current perceptions vividly capturing attention
- Paying attention to what stands out and is impactful
- Becoming aware of rich sensory details

- Noticing what's happening "now" as it changes
- Scanning the current situation for relevant information

- Energy going to more and new stimulation

- Focusing on possibilities for action
- Talking about things to do, actions to take
- Asking for specific details to perceive the pattern
- Reading minimal nonverbal cues
- Seeking aesthetic purity and pleasure in experiences
- Attention turning outward to more sensory input

- Living an experience

"This is what is."
"What's next?"

Extraverted iNtuiting N_e

—**Inferring**
—**Hypothesizing**
—**Seeing Potentials**
—**Wondering and Brainstorming**
—*Emergent*

- Current perceptions sparking alternatives
- Paying attention to relationships and connections
- Becoming aware of patterns, implications, and meanings
- Noticing meta-communications and what is not said
- Scanning the current situation for what might possibly be
- Energy going to interactions to generate more possibilities
- Focusing on multiple aspects of the whole context
- Talking about possibilities, new ideas, meanings
- Asking, "Have you thought about . . . ?"
- Reading the meanings of a situation
- Seeking more possibilities, ideas, options
- Attention turning outward to more relationships and meanings
- Interpreting an experience

"This is what might be."
"It could be this, or this, or this, or . . ."

Introverted Sensing S_i

—**Recalling**
—**Linking**
—**Comparing and Contrasting**
—**Noticing Match and Mismatch**
—*Past*

- Current perceptions eliciting stored impressions

- Paying attention to similarities and differences
- Becoming aware of differences from what was
- Noticing discrepancies
- Scanning memory bank for related information
- Energy staying with the recalled image
- Focusing on past successes (or failures)
- Talking about past experiences
- Asking for history or prior experience
- Reading lessons from the past
- Seeking to avoid mistakes made before
- Attention turning inward to images of past impressions

- Re-living an experience

"This is how it has always been."
"This reminds me of . . ."

Introverted iNtuiting N_i

—**Foreseeing**
—**Conceptualizing**
—**Understanding Complex Patterns**
—**Synthesizing and Symbolizing**
—*Future*

- Current perceptions sparking insights into complex situations
- Paying attention to future implications
- Becoming aware of universal meanings and symbols
- Noticing whole patterns or systems
- Scanning internal images for insights
- Energy staying with the vision
- Focusing on depth of understanding
- Talking about the future and the meaning
- Asking, "What is the goal?"
- Reading the future and the potential in others
- Seeking innovative ideas or universal symbols
- Attention turning inward to images forming of the future
- Imagining and anticipating an experience

"This is how it will be."
"Aha, that's it!"

THE PERCEIVING PROCESSES

Of What?

CONCRETE
(Sensory Information)

ABSTRACT
(Pattern Information)

HERE-AND-NOW
(Outside—The Extraverted World)

Where and When

**PAST, FUTURE
OR UNIVERSAL**
(Inside—The Introverted World)

Extraverted Sensing (S$_e$) *What is* Experience the experience	**Extraverted Intuiting (N$_e$)** *What it means* Conceive from the experience
Introverted Sensing (S$_i$) *What is evokes what was* Images from past experience or universal shared history	**Introverted Intuiting (N$_i$)** *What will be* Images of future or universal symbols

The perceiving process that is in the leading or supporting role indicates
the kinds of information we are most likely to seek and trust.

What kinds of information do you trust most?

What kinds of information do you tend to ignore or forget to seek out?

Your
PROBLEM SITUATION

**How might you have been overusing your preferred information-gathering
process in your problem situation?**

What action will you take to correct the situation?

Essential Characteristics of the Judging Processes

Extraverted Thinking — T$_e$

—Being Organized
—Coordinating and Sequencing
—Segmenting
—Checking Against Criteria
—*Particular to What Is Here and Now*

- Talking about the steps to get things done
- Asking Socratic questions to clarify logic or make a point
- Evaluating priorities in reaching a goal
- Deciding about sequence, hierarchy, schedule
- Determining the required resources to achieve a goal
- Being guided by organizing principles and criteria
- Convincing with logical arguments
- Noticing the component parts and what's missing
- Focusing on cause and effect
- Looking for logic
- Searching for efficient organization
- Seeking to establish order and efficiency
- Organizing an experience

"This is how to do it."
"People do . . ."

Extraverted Feeling — F$_e$

—Being Considerate
—Adjusting and Accommodating
—Affirming
—Checking Appropriateness
—*Particular to What Is Here and Now*

- Talking about personal details
- Asking questions to find out what others need

- Evaluating appropriateness
- Deciding about what is friendly, nice, mean
- Determining what others want
- Being guided by harmonizing the group
- Convincing with self-disclosure and warmth
- Noticing what's important to others
- Focusing on consideration of others
- Looking for unexpressed wants and needs
- Searching for connection and affirmation
- Seeking to establish rapport and stay in touch
- Relating through an experience

"This is what we need."
"We do . . ."

Introverted Thinking — T$_i$

—Principles
—Categorizing and Classifying
—Analyzing
—Checking Consistency
—*Universal*

- Asking what is wrong, how something's not working
- Looking for concise, clear explanations
- Evaluating accuracy and internal consistency
- Deciding what kind of object something is
- Determining the defining characteristics
- Being guided by the reasons things work
- Convincing with clear, precise definitions

- Noticing inconsistencies and imprecision
- Focusing on thorough analysis, seeing all the angles
- Talking about how things match a model or blueprint

- Searching for a "leverage point" to fix things
- Seeking to solve problems
- Analyzing and critiquing an experience

"This is why . . ."
"It does. . ."

Introverted Feeling — F$_i$

—Values
—Harmonizing and Clarifying
—Reconciling
—Checking Congruency
—*Universal*

- Talking about likes, dislikes, and what's important
- Asking, "Is it worth standing up for?"
- Evaluating priorities according to values
- Deciding about what is important
- Determining the essence of what's important
- Being guided by strong convictions
- Convincing with rightness-wrongness or goodness-badness
- Noticing incongruities and phoniness
- Focusing on authenticity, living out values
- Looking for intrinsic values, something worth believing in
- Searching for people, ideas, or actions worth promoting
- Seeking to establish loyalty and commitment
- Valuing an experience

"This is important."
"I (or you) do . . ."

THE JUDGING PROCESSES

Of What?

OBJECTIVE
(Order and Structure)

SUBJECTIVE
(Values and Worth)

HERE-AND-NOW
(Outside—The Extraverted World)

Where and When

**PAST, FUTURE
OR UNIVERSAL**
(Inside—The Introverted World)

Extraverted Thinking (T$_e$) *Organize the external world* *according to criteria* Organize the experience	**Extraverted Feeling (F$_e$)** *Arrange external world according* *to interpersonal importance* Relate to the experience
Introverted Thinking (T$_i$) *Check external events and ideas* *against internal framework* Analyze the experience	**Introverted Feeling (F$_i$)** *Check external events for* *congruence with internal values* Evaluate the experience

**The judging process that is in the leading or supporting role indicates
the kinds of decisions we tend to make easily and quickly.**

What kinds of decisions come easily to you?

What kinds of decisions do you avoid or put off?

Your
PROBLEM SITUATION

**How might you have been overusing your preferred judging process in your
problem situation?**

What action will you take to correct the situation?

The Extraverted Processes

All of the extraverted cognitive processes have in common that they are oriented to the present. There is a sense of immediacy—that the environment must be acted upon or responded to now. The focus of these processes is on breadth and "more." Using these processes we seek more information (S_e), more ideas (N_e), more relationships (F_e), or more order (T_e).

Roles of Your Extraverted Processes	Your Extraverted Processes
+ -	
+ -	
- +	
- +	

Our extraverted leading or supporting role process indicates the nature of an action we are likely to take in a situation without much consideration or effort.
(S_e—Experience, N_e—Infer, T_e—Organize, F_e—Accommodate)

Your
PROBLEM SITUATION

What actions did you take that got in the way of resolving the problem?

What action will you take to correct the situation?

The extraverted processes, no matter what role position, indicate ways we are likely to forge ahead without consideration.

Your
PROBLEM SITUATION

Did you simply *respond to what was happening* (S_e), *infer what someone meant* (N_e), *structure and organize* (T_e), or *accommodate and adjust* (F_e)?

What did you need to consider before you acted?

The Introverted Processes

All of the introverted cognitive processes have in common that they are oriented to a time or context outside the present—the past, the future, or a universal quality that transcends time. The focus of these processes is narrow and more focused on a singular "purpose." Introverted processes can either reference somthing personal or more universal experiences which generalize to many situations.

Roles of Your Introverted Processes	Your Introverted Processes
+ -	
+ -	
- +	
- +	

Our introverted leading or supporting role process indicates how we are likely to enter a situation—what kind of expectations we have going in to a situation. (S_i—Past Experiences, N_i—Vision, T_i—Models, F_i—Values)

Your
PROBLEM SITUATION

What expectations are getting in the way of your solving your problem situation?

What action will you take to correct the situation?

The introverted processes, no matter what their role position, indicate ways we are likely to resist change.

The introverted processes are often taken for granted. What is perceived or judged seems "locked in" and has an enduring quality since it does not vary with the situation as in the extraverted processes. To make matters worse, we often don't find the words to adequately express the richness of what is perceived or judged through the introverted processes. Others don't see what we see, feel what we feel, or know what we know through these processes, and sometimes only hear about them when they "bump into them."

Your
PROBLEM SITUATION

Are you stuck in *the way things were* (S_i), *a vision of the future* (N_i), *absolute principles* (T_i), or *dogmatic values* (F_i)?
How do you need to be more open?

Do you need to be more expressive and take time to articulate something?

Your Relief(+)/Unsettling(-) Role Process

Our relief role process can give us a
sense of other abilities we have developed.
It can also give us a way out of being stuck
and to find a source of balance.

Your
PROBLEM SITUATION

Is this process proving to
be unsettling in your
problem situation?

How might you use this process to get out
of overusing your leading or supporting
role processes?

Your Aspirational(+)/Projective(-) Role Process

Our aspirational role process indicates a way
we might act negatively under stress
as we project onto others the negative
qualities we don't like in ourselves.

Your
PROBLEM SITUATION

Are you projecting your own
weaknesses into the situation?

What unrealistic standards have you
established?

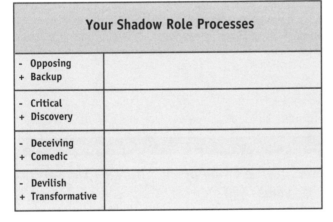

Your Shadow Role Processes	
- Opposing + Backup	
- Critical + Discovery	
- Deceiving + Comedic	
- Devilish + Transformative	

Our opposing role process indicates what we
are likely to be adamant about.

The other shadow role processes are likely to be
blind spots, yet they can be great resources.

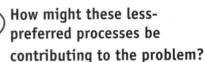

Your
PROBLEM SITUATION

How might these less-
preferred processes be
contributing to the problem?

How might they provide a resource for a
solution to the problem?

Some Important Problem-Solving and Communication Principles:

- Develop and trust your leading role and supporting role processes. This is how you were designed to operate.
- Chances are, you will be naturally attracted to situations where those processes are appropriate and effective.
- When you get stuck, find a way to engage your relief role process. It should provide a way out of being stuck.
- For important decisions, consciously engage as many processes as you can. Find friends, family, or coworkers who can help you fill in the gaps and suggest aspects you might not have considered.
- When you want to consciously engage an introverted process, you may need to set aside time to be alone.
- When you want to consciously engage an extraverted process, seek out the company of others.
- Be open to input from all sources.
- Be patient with yourself and know that when you have to use a less-preferred process, it will take more energy.

> As you begin to use your new understanding of the cognitive processes, you may notice some confusing similarities. Use the following information to help you sort out the differences among them.

Look-Alikes and Differentiators

Introverted Sensing and introverted Feeling are often associated with a strong kinesthetic sense—like a whole body feeling-tone response. Remember, introverted Sensing is an information source that informs decisions. When engaging in this process, a series of past impressions comes to mind unbidden. Introverted Feeling is a judging process that uses different sources of information as checkpoints along the way to know if the evaluation is "right."

Introverted Thinking and introverted iNtuiting are often accompanied by a sense of detachment and disconnection. With both there tends to be comfort with complexity. The difference is that when we are engaging in introverted Thinking, we usually have a clear sense of the principles or models something is judged against, whereas with introverted iNtuiting, an impressionistic image forms in the mind.

Extraverted Sensing and extraverted Thinking are often used when there is a focus on facts and an empirical approach. Keep in mind that extraverted Sensing is a perceptive process and may consist of data gathering with questions, whereas extraverted Thinking is a judging process in which the purpose of questions is to establish logic.

Extraverted iNtuiting and extraverted Feeling often focus on people and their interactions. With extraverted iNtuiting, it is the meanings and inferences that come to mind relative to people and their interactions. With extraverted Feeling, it is the actions that keep people connected or disconnected that matter.

Extraverted Sensing and extraverted iNtuiting are both simultaneous in nature and involve perception of many things at once. This can lead to random activity as the outer world is scanned for additional information. With extraverted Sensing, there is an emphasis on possibilities for actions to take. With extraverted iNtuiting, there is an emphasis on possibilities to be *considered* for action.

Introverted Sensing and introverted iNtuiting are both more focused and involve perception of "one thing at a time." This gives the behavior a sequential appearance, with a sense of beginning, middle, and end. With introverted Sensing, the sequence is often logistical in nature and based on the past. Introverted iNtuiting is based on a vision for the future, and the focus is on what steps to take next.

The similarities, differences, and interactional qualities of the processes can lead to some confusion about our preferences as we try to determine our best-fit type, and yet they provide a richness to our behavior that we must not lose.

> The following brief descriptions portray the typical problem-solving and decision making styles of each of the sixteen types. Use them to understand yourself, to understand others, and to improve your interactions with others.

Foreseer Developer • INFJ

Decisions are made quickly if the information matches their impressions, and slowly if new information must be integrated into their understanding of the people system. They gather personal information, including global impressions, feelings, and emotional tone, comparing them to impressions and symbolic meaning. Decisions are most often based on impact on the people in the system. Inaction may result when they have no idea of the next step or they are overwhelmed with the physical realities of a situation. To influence them, show them another perspective and talk about the future and how a decision will affect others. Give them time to integrate new information into their vision and their models of how things will be.

Harmonizer Clarifier • INFP

They quickly decide if something or someone is congruent, yet decide slowly regarding actions to take. They are generally quite aware of implications and meanings of different actions, so they may vacillate until they are sure values are not violated. They gather personal information, including global impressions and feeling-tones. Inaction may result if personal values conflict with external demands for action and many differing values have to be reconciled and unified in one decision. They tend to take in a lot of information and play with a lot of ideas, yet may act on impulse once values are aligned. To influence them, show them how new options are congruent with deep values.

Envisioner Mentor • ENFJ

Most decisions are made quickly except when they are not ready to make a decision. They gather personal information, including global impressions, feelings, and emotional tone. They need an opportunity to generate possibilities toward a plan. They will withdraw mentally to visualize the impact of the new information on the people involved. They often base decisions on what is most fitting and suitable according to the values of the group. When a decision is based on strong values regarding what is right for themselves, they may be very hard to influence. Give them reflection time to sort through everything and readjust their vision. To influence them, show them how a decision will affect others or how boundaries have been breached.

Discoverer Advocate • ENFP

They make quick decisions in response to opportunities that match the "ideal," or may deliberate over choosing the one right thing. They can get overwhelmed by all the options they see if not thoroughly in touch with their values. They generate possibilities based on the global impressions, feelings, and emotional tones they read in the situation. They respond to their immediate impressions and will either take action accordingly, or put off deciding if personal values are not evoked. Decisions are based on what is individually and universally important. To influence them, show them another perspective or option that will be good for people and does not go against their values.

Conceptualizer Director • INTJ

Strategic decisions come quickly as they compare new information to their abstract representations of the universe. Concrete, logistical decisions often frustrate them or go unmade. They gather lots of information to base decisions on the "how" and "why" in terms of effectiveness. Their focus is on future applications and progress. An impersonal approach is usually taken. To influence their decisions, present a logical argument about long-range implications, build a new premise for their logic, and give them time and space to see where it fits in their framework. They may need to reconceptualize their whole system if what you propose is too different from their vision.

Designer Theorizer • INTP

They quickly decide on the accuracy of theories and frameworks, yet labor over accurate expression of ideas. They may avoid decisions regarding an action or establishing order and structure. They gather conceptual information to sort into categories, and may not act until guiding principles are clear. Their focus is on accuracy of the theory and clarity of the model. Logistical decisions are seen as trivial and either slighted or labored over. Interpersonal decisions are made to avoid disruption and to keep the peace. To influence them, give them new information presenting other workable options. Be sure there is internal consistency in your logic, and be prepared for mutual critique and debate.

Strategist Mobilizer • ENTJ

Most decisions are fast and seemingly impersonal. They gather conceptual and factual information to make their vision happen and find what is motivating. They orient to the external world quickly, and pick up information that helps them make simultaneous assessments of a multitude of data points. They easily make decisions based on the organization and implementation of their strategy. To influence their decisions, present a logical argument about long-range implications and effectiveness. Don't confuse their decisiveness with being inflexible. They will quickly reprioritize so as to not waste time on things that won't get desired results. You may need to build a new premise for their logic and let them think about it.

Explorer Inventor • ENTP

They are quick to infer and read a situation. They make decisions quickly in response to new information regarding the system or the potential for making a complex model accessible and usable. They are hesitant when there is no strategy or when relationships are at risk. They quickly gather conceptual information to sort into categories, set criteria, and move to a metaposition with principles about how to problem-solve. Decisions are based first on new possibilities that will get the job done, and then on theoretical accuracy. They like having multiple models to use as guiding principles. To influence them, give them new information, another idea, and other options that will lead to improvement. Be prepared for a devil's advocate argument.

Planner Inspector • ISTJ

They decide quickly when they believe they understand the situation. When the situation is unfamiliar, they seek first to relate it to their previous experience, then make a cautious decision. Once a decision is made, it is not easily changed unless shown to be impractical. They like concrete facts more than hypothetical implications. They usually base their decisions on keeping order and completing tasks. To be influenced, they need lots of information to compare to their large data bank of life experiences and stored information. Give them factual information, in writing, early in the decision-making process. Then leave them alone to plan and reflect so they can determine the necessary logistical preparations.

Protector Supporter • ISFJ

They generally make slow, careful decisions that usually stick unless there is a negative impact on someone they care about. They like lots of information and filter it through a large data bank of life experiences and stored information, looking for what is familiar. They want concrete facts that impact harmony and how the decision will affect the people they know by helping them or interfering. They want to be supportive and make sure things go right. Sometimes decisions will be made "by the book" in a conventional way just to reach closure. To influence them, give them information early in the decision-making process, then leave them alone to analyze it. Show them how it will be helpful to people.

Implementor Supervisor • ESTJ

They make task decisions quickly, but may make life decisions slowly if they have no conventional examples to follow. They pay attention to concrete facts and compare them to a large internal data bank of life experiences and stored information, as well as external rules and standards. They like lots of organized information when something new is being considered. Decisions are usually based on criteria for keeping order and completing tasks and the responsible thing to do. To influence, give them organized, factual information, preferably in writing, early in the decision process. Then suggest how all of it connects to their experiences.

Facilitator Caretaker • ESFJ

They often make quick decisions for the welfare of others. Task decisions are made quickly if direction and sequence are clear but may be changed if a new decision will be more helpful. They tend to research a great deal, seeking concrete facts to compare to their large data bank of personal experiences and stored information, especially about people. Their focus is on keeping harmony and considering how decisions will affect people they know and care about. They often take on too much and ignore their own needs. To influence them, give them information in person or verbally, especially about the impact on people, and then give them time to reflect and analyze the situation.

Analyzer Operator • ISTP

They decide quickly when responding to immediate need, but slowly when they don't see options for action. They're constantly observing, taking in a lot of concrete information and looking for all the angles. They like to see if the facts fit together, try something, and see what happens. They respond to the needs of the moment when new information comes in that will make something work more efficiently, but prefer to enter a situation having analyzed it first. To influence them, give them the rationale for the change that is needed and move them to some kind of action. Then discuss the results of that action. Let them know there is a problem for them to solve.

Composer Producer • ISFP

They seem to vacillate between slow decisions and quick action. They constantly check against their values and tend to adjust their actions as the situation changes to keep true to what is important. This can look like constantly changing their minds, especially if no immediate action is taken on an earlier decision. They tend to base actions on what is happening in the immediate external world that is relevant and try to stick with what's important and what will make something better. They get a strong sense of what is needed and try various approaches until the desired result is achieved. To influence them, acknowledge what is important to them and to others in a mutually beneficial way. Show how it will get the desired result.

Promoter Executor • ESTP

They make fast decisions that are realistic and pragmatic. They rapidly take in the currently-available concrete information. They may look like they take in little, but the information is rich in detail and comes all at once. Then they move quickly to action. They base decisions on what is happening in the immediate external world that gets their attention as relevant to getting the job done. To influence them, let them experience the change, try a different angle, or shift their perspective. Let them know there is some urgency. They are not easily influenced by abstract explanations, but more by what impact their actions will have, and a respectful, confident, and positive attitude toward them.

Motivator Presenter • ESFP

They generally make decisions quickly about what action to take, but may vary the decision when new options for action are seen. They take in a lot of rich detail, noticing minimal nonverbal cues. They are responsive to the needs of the immediate situation, especially regarding people and their reactions. They base decisions on what is important in relation to what is happening in the immediate external world. They automatically attend to what will make people satisfied, and seek to help them do what they want to do. To influence them, join them in figuring out what else to try and show how it is relevant and important. Let them know what you like and want and how they can help.

Understanding your pattern of using the cognitive processes is key to improving your communication.

Communication

You cannot not communicate. Everything we do or don't do communicates something. Each of the cognitive processes is associated with different kinds of communication. Once you are aware of your own preferred processes, you can begin to notice how your preferences influence how and what you communicate. You can also identify how these preferences may be a source of misunderstanding and conflict.

Think back on your problem situation or different communication. What was said? What was not said, but implied? What was the nature of the misunderstanding or miscommunication? Refer back to pages 37–39 and identify which processes you seemed to be using the most in this situation. Use the following chart to locate the source of the misunderstanding. Did you overuse or not use the process?

The Eight Cognitive Processes and Communication/Miscommunication

	Your Communication Difficulty		
INFORMATION-ACCESSING PROCESSES (Perception)	didn't use	appropriate use	over use
S$_e$—Experiencing and noticing the physical world, scanning for visible reactions and relevant data Being attracted to and/or distracted by changing external events. Adapting and changing your mind according to the situation. Focusing on facts. Asking lots of questions to get enough information to see the pattern. Going ahead and responding to raw data. Physical self-expression.			
S$_i$—Recalling past experiences, remembering detailed data and what it is linked to Being heavily influenced by prior experiences. Distrusting new information that doesn't match. Assuming an understanding of a situation because it resembles a prior one. Focusing on facts and stored data. Giving lots of specific, sequential details about something. Rating and making comparison.			
N$_e$—Inferring relationships, noticing threads of meaning, and scanning for what could be Being attracted to new ideas and possible realities. Holding different and even conflicting ideas and values in mind at once without articulating them. Assuming a meaning of something. Focusing on inferences and hypotheses. Extemporaneously connecting ideas.			
N$_i$—Foreseeing implications, conceptualizing, and having images of the future or profound meaning Being strongly influenced by a vision of what will be, which may involve an abstract, even vague understanding of complexities that are difficult to explain. Focusing on a preconceived outcome or goal. Perhaps not articulating or even aware of premises or assumptions behind envisioned implications. Describing implications and the final picture.			
EVALUATING PROCESSES (Judgment)	didn't use	appropriate use	over use
T$_e$—Organizing, segmenting, sorting, and applying logic and criteria Expressing thoughts directly, readily critiquing and pointing out what has been left out or not done. Getting to the point efficiently and getting the task done. Taking decisive action, which may be misread as closed mindedness. Focusing on logic and criteria for setting up systems of organization.			
T$_i$—Analyzing, categorizing, and figuring out how something works Defining principles, differences and distinctions. Pointing out inconsistencies and critiquing inaccuracies. Engaging in detached observation which can be misread as dislike or disapproval. Not expressing thoughts unless illogic and inaccuracy are overwhelming. Focusing on identifying, analyzing, naming, and categorizing.			
F$_e$—Considering others and responding to them Expressing positive and negative feelings openly. Disclosing personal details to establish rapport. Pointing out how to attend to needs of others and complaining when others are not considerate. Expressing of warmth, caring and concern and interest in others, which can be misread as suffocating or not attending to a task. Focusing on appropriateness and connectedness.			
F$_i$—Evaluating importance and maintaining congruence Clarifying what is important. Pointing out contradictions and incongruities between actions and espoused values. Expressing quiet reserve, which is often misread as aloofness. Adamantly insisting on what is important, or what you want or like. Not expressing inner convictions unless important values are comprised.			

Communication and Relationships

Communication and problem solving occur in the context of relationships. When there is a problem, it is helpful to sort out the various ways people are different from each other, and to find ways they can connect.

List your pattern, then list their pattern. Draw lines to show where your leading and supporting role processes are in their pattern. Do the same in reverse for relating their pattern to yours. Draw a dotted line to show where you connect with your relief role processes.

Once you know your pattern of cognitive processes, you can compare yours to others' and see just where the communication zone is.

Here is an example

Roles of the Processes	Your Pattern of Processes INTP	the Communication Zone™	Their Pattern of Processes ISFP
+ Leading 1st – Dominating	T_i		F_i
+ Supporting 2nd – Overprotective	N_e		S_e
+ Relief 3rd – Unsettling	S_i		N_i
+ Aspirational 4th – Projective	F_e		T_e
– Opposing 5th + Backup	T_e		F_e
– Critical 6th + Discovery	N_i		S_i
– Deceiving 7th + Comedic	S_e		N_e
– Devilish 8th + Transformative	F_i		T_i

Communication between these two people is loaded with "land mines." There is a tremendous difference in the information they access and the way they reach conclusions. An interaction can easily trigger the negative sides of both their processes.

Does this mean that miscommunication is unavoidable? No. It simply means that these two people need to spend time in dialog in order to understand and clarify the other person's perspective. Effective communication is likely to happen when they take time to listen to each other and value the differences each contributes to the dialog. If they have common goals and objectives, they will be motivated to make the effort. The rewards they stand to reap will be substantial because of the diverse cognitive processes they bring to the situation.

Some options when there is no match above the shadow zone

- Seek mediation from a third person who shares some of each of your preferences.
- Give up! (Probably not the choice you want to make.)
- Acknowledge the gap and agree to work hard at the communication.
- Use it as an opportunity to grow.
- Find another level to connect on—shared values, talents, desired outcomes, family ties, or friendships.
- Rejoice in your diversity.
- Try to avoid confrontation, especially when you are tired or stressed.

Another Example, Another Challenge

In the following relationship example, communication is likely to be easy at first, and a great deal of energy will be present in the relationship as they generate possibilities and new ideas and see potential. At the same time, there is a danger of making assumptions that they are communicating about the same information. The quite different judging processes can "direct" a focus toward different inferences. Interactions can also easily trigger the negative side of the other's processes as well, since the leading role of one is the devilish role of the other. Shared past experiences (S_i) can serve to get them out of gridlock. There can be blind spots about what is happening in the real world (S_e).

Roles of the Processes	Your Pattern of Processes INTP	the Communication Zone™	Their Pattern of Processes INFP
+ Leading 1st - Dominating	T_i		F_i
+ Supporting 2nd - Overprotective	N_e		N_e
+ Relief 3rd - Unsettling	S_i		S_i
+ Aspirational 4th - Projective	F_e		T_e
- Opposing 5th + Backup	T_e		F_e
- Critical 6th + Discovery	N_i		N_i
- Deceiving 7th + Comedic	S_e		Se
- Devilish 8th + Transformative	F_i		T_i

If we only know the negative side of the cognitive processes in ourselves, we are inclined to reject the positive side in others.

REMEMBER

The more you apply your understanding of the cognitive processes to your own problem solving and communication, the more you stand to learn. If you do not engage a needed process easily, and you have no idea how to approach your problem or communication using it, seek out someone for whom that process plays a leading or supporting role and use them as a coach.

The responsibility for the communication is on the person with a vested interest in the outcome of the communication. If that is you, then your task is to flex your communication, try to reach the other person where they are, and find a way to connect. In the end, it's worth it!

Another Example, Yet Another Challenge

This communication zone predicts ease of communication. However, if the models that are held in introverted Thinking are not shared, there can be constant critiquing of each other's models and decisions. The major problem with this relationship is likely to be shared blind spots. A positive benefit is that the relationship may push the two people to develop the other sides of themselves.

> "Two people who prefer the same kinds of perception and judgment have the best chance of understanding each other and feeling understood."
> —Isabell Briggs Myers*

Roles of the Processes		Your Pattern of Processes INTP	the Communication Zone™	Their Pattern of Processes INTP
+ Leading - Dominating	1st	T_i		T_i
+ Supporting - Overprotective	2nd	N_e		N_e
+ Relief - Unsettling	3rd	S_i		S_i
+ Aspirational - Projective	4th	F_e		F_e
- Opposing + Backup	5th	T_e		T_e
- Critical + Discovery	6th	N_i		N_i
- Deceiving + Comedic	7th	S_e		Se
- Devilish + Transformative	8th	F_i		F_i

When a match is predicted but doesn't happen—

- See if past experiences are presenting roadblocks and work to clear them up.
- Look at the current situation to see if core values and needs are at stake.
- Consider that one person or both have not yet developed one of their "preferred" cognitive process and have no skill in using it.
- Consider that there is a stress response, and one or both are stuck in the negative role of the process.

Effective communication results when we are open to working through our diverse perspectives. Each cognitive process brings different premises to our conversations. True dialog occurs when we can suspend hasty or dogmatic perception and judgment. In the ideal situation, we may hope to bridge our differences just by knowing about how others are different and therefore being more open. The reality is, this may not happen by itself. We tend to reject the positive aspects of our less-preferred cognitive processes because our experience of them is so negative. For example, Mary's leading role process is introverted Thinking. She experiences introverted Feeling most often in its negative aspect of the devilish role with a somewhat childish, "I want . . . ," rather than a more mature, "This is what is important." When she began working with someone for whom introverted Feeling was a leading role process, she experienced him as dogmatic, unyielding, and off target rather than as someone who was tuned in to values that could help them prioritize their projects and better accomplish their goals. It was only when she started recognizing her own projections and taking her own wants and values more seriously that she became open to her coworker's contributions.

Six Steps to Understanding Your Communication Zone

What do you like/dislike about the person? Review the descriptions of their cognitive processes.

1. **List your best-fit pattern of processes in the left column.** (see p. 34)

2. **List the pattern of processes of the person in your problem situation in the right column.** (see p. 32)

Is what you like or dislike related to one of their cognitive processes? If so, how can you be more accepting of and actually appreciate the person?

3. **Draw lines from your leading and supporting role processes to where those processes fall in their pattern.**

4. **Draw lines to show where their leading and supporting role processes are in your pattern.**

Is what you dislike a projection of your own blind spots? If so, seek to find some value in that aspect of the person, and allow yourself to be less proficient in that area.

5. **Draw a dotted line to show where you connect with your relief role processes.**

6. **Answer the questions to the right.**

Is what you admire in the person what you need to develop in yourself? Would this person make a good coach or role model for you?

"A real understanding can, in my view, be reached only when the diversity of psychological premises is accepted."
—Carl Jung*

Roles of the Processes	Your Pattern of Processes _ _ _ _	✦ the Communication Zone™		Their Pattern of Processes _ _ _ _
+ Leading 1st - Dominating				
+ Supporting 2nd - Overprotective				
+ Relief 3rd - Unsettling				
+ Aspirational 4th - Projective				
- Opposing 5th + Backup				
- Critical 6th + Discovery				
- Deceiving 7th + Comedic				
- Devilish 8th + Transformative				

* Carl G. Jung, *Psychological Types* (Princeton, N.J., Princeton University Press, 1995), 489.

Development

Each personality type pattern predicts a likely pattern of emerging development. In other words, there seems to be a time frame when we are naturally prompted to develop the leading role process, the supporting role process, the relief role process, and the aspirational role process. While there is much possible variation in the sequence of development, we generally expect the leading role process to develop first, and evidence of this development can usually be observed in early childhood. Then, along about the beginning of adolescence, interests shift and there seems to be a natural push to develop the supporting role process. No wonder adolescence is so full of changes, with the shift in personality development as well as raging hormones and school and social changes! But that's not enough change. Just about the time we begin to face being on our own in young adulthood, we find ourselves drawn to activities associated with the relief role process. About middle adulthood, just when we tend to have our family and careers well underway, we often face another developmental urge to grow and develop our aspirational role process.

These developmental time frames are easily influenced by our life circumstances. Often when our environment doesn't foster and allow the development of our preferred processes, we may overdevelop one or skip one entirely. The basic guideline is that indeed we do develop and engage the different processes in response to life's demands.

By now you have a sense of which cognitive processes you have easy access to and have developed some skill in. As you reflect on where you are now in your life—your age and your past experiences—what cognitive process are you developing now? What do you need to develop next? What do you see yourself developing in the future?

Where Are You in Your Development?

Your Best-Fit Pattern of Cognitive Processes (from p. 34)

___ ___ ___ ___ ___ ___ ___ ___

What cognitive processes have you already developed?

Ask yourself these questions:
- Has my family background presented me with challenges and opportunities for development, or with roadblocks?
- Does my culture and social situation confront me with possible roadblocks or challenges?
- Does my job or workstyle stifle or foster my development?
- Do my current relationships present demands that require extra energy or create a void in my life?

What cognitive process(es) are you developing now?

Guidelines for development:
- Be open to opportunities to grow.
- Find a role model who has a certain process well developed and spend time with him or her.
- Change your environment if possible.
- Educate yourself and be patient with yourself.
- Rejoice in who you are naturally.

Remember, you are freer to be who you are not, once you know and accept who you are.

Essential Qualities of the Patterns

Temperament

(For a complete explanation of Temperament Theory see: *Understanding Yourself and Others, An Introduction to Temperament.*)

Four Patterns

Each of the sixteen type patterns can be understood in several important ways.

The types are clustered into four groups. These are broad themes, called temperament. Temperament speaks to a pattern of core psychological needs, core values, talents, and behaviors—all of which are interrelated. The four temperaments also have qualities in common with each other and can be described in those terms as well.

	ABSTRACT	CONCRETE
AFFILIATIVE	**IDEALIST** ABSTRACT/AFFILIATIVE Meaning and Significance Unique Identity DIPLOMATIC—clarifying, unifying, individualizing, and inspiring	**GUARDIAN** CONCRETE/AFFILIATIVE Membership or Belonging Responsibility or Duty LOGISTICAL—organizing, facilitating, checking, and supporting
PRAGMATIC	**RATIONAL** ABSTRACT/PRAGMATIC Mastery and Self-Control Knowledge and Competence STRATEGIC—engineering, conceptualizing, theorizing, and coordinating	**ARTISAN** CONCRETE/PRAGMATIC Freedom to Act Ability to Make an Impact TACTICAL—actions, composing, producing, and motivating

Interaction Styles
Four Patterns to Eight

Each of the four temperament patterns is expressed in either a *Directing* style or an *Informing* style.

The *Directing* interaction style has a time and task focus with a tendency to direct the actions of others in order to accomplish the task in accordance with deadlines, often by either "telling" or "asking." Regarding motivations and process, the *Directing* style is explicit.

The opposite style is *Informing*, with a motivation and process focus. Using this style, people tend to give information in order to enroll others into the process. When a task needs to be accomplished, the informing style engages others, describing outcomes and processes that can be used to complete the task.

Each style has its own best and appropriate use, and most people use both at different times but have more comfort with one. Each temperament pattern is differentiated by a preference for using one of these styles, giving us the eight patterns suggested by the matrix below.

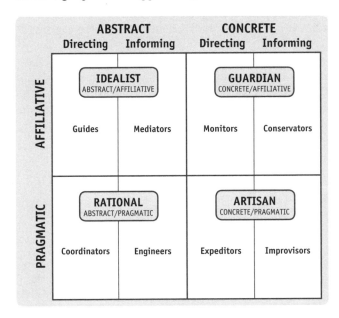

		ABSTRACT		CONCRETE	
		Directing	Informing	Directing	Informing
AFFILIATIVE		**IDEALIST** ABSTRACT/AFFILIATIVE		**GUARDIAN** CONCRETE/AFFILIATIVE	
		Guides	Mediators	Monitors	Conservators
PRAGMATIC		**RATIONAL** ABSTRACT/PRAGMATIC		**ARTISAN** CONCRETE/PRAGMATIC	
		Coordinators	Engineers	Expeditors	Improvisors

Eight Patterns to Sixteen

Each of these patterns can also be further differentiated by another dimension—a preference for either *Initiating* interactions and a faster pace, or for *Responding* to interactions and a slower pace. Now we have sixteen patterns, each with a "theme" as in the matrix below.

		ABSTRACT		CONCRETE	
		Directing	Informing	Directing	Informing
AFFILIATIVE	Responding	Chart the Course	Behind the Scenes	Chart the Course	Behind the Scenes
		IDEALIST ABSTRACT/AFFILIATIVE		**GUARDIAN** CONCRETE/AFFILIATIVE	
	Initiating	In Charge	Get Things Going	In Charge	Get Things Going
PRAGMATIC	Responding	Chart the Course	Behind the Scenes	Chart the Course	Behind the Scenes
		RATIONAL ABSTRACT/PRAGMATIC		**ARTISAN** CONCRETE/PRAGMATIC	
	Initiating	In Charge	Get Things Going	In Charge	Get Things Going

Overall, the interaction styles refer to how we typically interact with others. Interaction styles have been described by many in the field of personality and are also frequently described as social styles. The behaviors can be highly situational, but the styles are also inborn patterns that are revealed in the sixteen type patterns.

How Do Jung and Keirsey Relate?

David Keirsey's temperament patterns (extended out to the four variations of each) meet Jung's theory at the level of the sixteen type patterns. The four-letter code produced by the MBTI stands for one of sixteen type patterns. When it is accurate and verified for the individual, it matches one of Keirsey's sixteen type patterns. While at first glance the matching process looks illogical, it matches at a deep theoretical level when comparing the theoretical underpinnings of each—Jung for the MBTI and Ernst Kretschmer for Keirsey's temperaments. More importantly, it matches on a descriptive, behavioral level.

	ABSTRACT		CONCRETE	
	Directing	Informing	Directing	Informing
AFFILIATIVE / Responding	Foreseer Developer INFJ	Harmonizer Clarifier INFP	Planner Inspector ISTJ	Protector Supporter ISFJ
Initiating	**IDEALIST** ABSTRACT/AFFILIATIVE		**GUARDIAN** CONCRETE/AFFILIATIVE	
	Envisioner Mentor ENFJ	Discoverer Advocate ENFP	Implementor Supervisor ESTJ	Facilitator Caretaker ESFJ
PRAGMATIC / Responding	Conceptualizer Director INTJ	Designer Theorizer INTP	Analyzer Operator ISTP	Composer Producer ISFP
Initiating	**RATIONAL** ABSTRACT/PRAGMATIC		**ARTISAN** CONCRETE/PRAGMATIC	
	Strategist Mobilizer ENTJ	Explorer Inventor ENTP	Promoter Executor ESTP	Motivator Presenter ESFP

Temperament and the MBTI Code

Given the organizing principles of the temperament patterns of needs, values and talents, we like to use the following explanation to link Jung's theory with the four temperaments.

The eight cognitive processes described by Jung are used to meet the needs and promote the values of the temperament pattern. Certain of these processes suit the pattern so well that the preference for these processes match the preferences indicated by the four letter MBTI codes as follows:

Artisan   _S_P

Artisans can meet their needs for impact and freedom best through the process of extraverted Sensing. This process keeps them tuned in to the needs of the moment and they can readily take tactical actions and seize opportunities. How else would you recognize an opportunity? Thus all Artisans have S and P in their codes. Directing Artisans have S, T, and P in their codes and Informing Artisans have S, F, and P in their codes.

Guardian   _S_J

Guardians can meet their needs for membership and responsibility best through the process of introverted Sensing. They make sure the world will go on by referencing what has gone before. Their vast data bank of stored images and impressions informs the decisions they need to make to preserve the community through logistical actions. All Guardians have S and J in their codes. Directing Guardians have S, T, and J in their codes and Informing Guardians have S, F, and J in their codes.

Rational   _NT_

Rationals meet their needs for knowledge and competence through the mental processes of iNtuiting and Thinking—both in the extraverted and introverted mode. The organizing frameworks and models of the Thinking judgment process used with iNtuiting allow them to readily comprehend complex subjects without experiencing and memorizing, which is time consuming. Since they are dealing with the world of theories and strategy, they prefer objective decisions. All Rationals have N and T in their codes. Directing Rationals have N, T, and J in their codes and Informing Rationals have N, T, and P in their codes.

Idealist   _NF_

Idealists meet their needs for meaning and identity through the mental processes of iNtuiting and Feeling—both in the extraverted and introverted mode. Both Feeling judgment processes give them ways to act that are congruent with higher purposes in life (one's own and others'). It is only through examination of the meaning and the pattern information provided by the iNtuiting process that they can apprehend what will be or what is significant in the long run. All Idealists have N and F in their codes. Directing Idealists have N, F, and J in their codes and Informing Idealists have N, F, and P in their codes.

"Cracking the Code"

It is important to remember that the four-letter type code is more than the sum of four letters. It results from how we answer questions along four dichotomies, Extraversion-Introversion, Sensing-iNtuiting, Thinking-Feeling, and Judging-Perceiving. While on the surface each of these dichotomies can be described generally, they are not separate parts or traits. In the development of the MBTI, it was assumed that reporting preferences for one over the other of each dichotomy would give us an idea of the pattern of cognitive processes of the personality and thus reveal Jung's psychological type patterns. Use the following diagram to remind you of the kinds of processes and what the letters mean.

One can "crack the code" in a mechanical fashion and for some people this is necessary for them to understand how the processes are in a hierarchy.

What follows is a step-by-step process for converting the MBTI code to the pattern of processes represented by that code.

1. **Look at the last letter of the code. It tells you which one of the two middle letters is extraverted**
   If it is J, then that tells you that the T or F in the code is used in the external world.

   • TJ in the code indicates extraverted Thinking is the preferred process of judgment for that type pattern.

   • FJ in the code indicates extraverted Feeling is the preferred process of judgment for that type pattern.

   Some people say that J "points to" the letter just next to it.

   If it is P, then that tells you that the S or N in the code is used in the external world.

   • S_P in the code indicates extraverted Sensing is the preferred process of perception for that type pattern.

   • N_P in the code indicates extraverted iNtuiting is the preferred process of perception for that type pattern.

   Some people say that P "points to" the previous letter.

Jung's Cognitive Processes as They Appear in the Four-Letter Personality Type Code

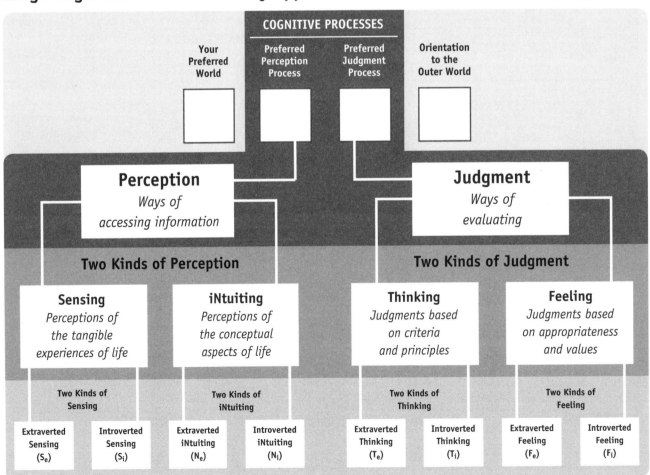

2. **Now that you have determined which process is extraverted, know that the remaining middle letter in the code is introverted.**

3. **Now look at the first letter in the code.**
   If it is an E, then the extraverted process identified in step one is the leading role process (dominant).
   If it is an I, then the introverted process identified in step two is the leading role process (dominant).

4. **The other middle letter is the supporting role process (auxiliary).**

5. **The dichotomous opposite of the supporting role process will be the relief role process (tertiary).**

6. **The dichotomous opposite of the leading role process will be the aspirational role process (inferior).**

7. **To get the shadow processes, just take the hierarchical sequence of the primary processes and reverse the attitude (extraverted or introverted) of the process.**

REMEMBER: The Judging/Perceiving dichotomy is the key to understanding the *pattern of cognitive processes* of a given personality type code.

"CRACKING THE CODE"

Steps	Example 1	Example 2	Example 3	Example 4

I. Note the processes (S, N, T, F) in your 4-letter code AND the processes not shown in your 4-letter code.	I N T J
	  S F
		E S T P
		  N F
			I N F P
			  S T
				E S F J
				  N T

II. Identify your orientation to the external world.
 	
First, complete steps 1 OR 2.
 	
1. If your 4-letter code has a J — place an $_e$ next to your T or F.
 	
2. If your 4-letter code has a P — place an $_e$ next to your S or N.
 	
Now, complete steps 3 OR 4.
 	
3. If your 4-letter code has T_e or F_e
  • put $_i$ next to the S or N in your 4-letter code and
  • put $_i$ next to the T or F not shown in your 4-letter code and
  • put $_e$ next to the S or N not shown in your 4-letter code.
 	
4. If your 4-letter code has S_e or N_e
  • put $_i$ next to T or F in your 4-letter code and
  • put $_i$ next to the S or N not shown in your 4-letter code and
  • put $_e$ next to the T or F not shown in your 4-letter code.
	I N T_e J
	  S F
	
	I N_i T_e J
	  S_e F_i
		E S_e T P
		  N F
		
		E S_e T_i P
		  N_i F_e
			I N_e F P
			  S T
			
			I N_e F_i P
			  S_i T_e
				E S F_e J
				  N T
				
				E S_i F_e J
				  N_e T_i

III. Identify your dominant process.
Complete steps 1 OR 2.
 	
1. If your 4-letter code has E—then your dominant process is the process with $_e$.
 	
2. If your 4-letter code has I—then your dominant process is the process with $_i$.
	I $\boxed{N_i}$ T_e J
	  S_e F_i
		E $\boxed{S_e}$ T_i P
		  N_i F_e
			I N_e $\boxed{F_i}$ P
			  S_i T_e
				E S_i $\boxed{F_e}$ J
				  N_e T_i

IV. Identify your hierarchy of processes.
Complete steps 1 OR 2.
 	
1. If your dominant process is T or F—your hierarchical sequence is counter clockwise starting from your dominant process.
 	
2. If your dominant process is S or N—your hierarchical sequence is clockwise starting from your dominant process.
	I $\boxed{N_i}$ T_e J
	  S_e F_i
		E $\boxed{S_e}$ T_i P
		  N_i F_e
			I N_e $\boxed{F_i}$ P
			  S_i T_e
				E S_i $\boxed{F_e}$ J
				  N_e T_i

Notes for the Facilitator

Purpose

This booklet was developed to introduce Jung's concepts, as well as offer some practical applications. Its content can form the basis of a half- to one-day workshop to enrich the self-discovery process. Several departures from the standard introduction of type are contained in this booklet. As a facilitator or someone who is already familiar with type and the MBTI, you may want to know more about why the facilitators trained by Temperament Reasearch Institute present type this way.

Where to Start

We have found that we are more effective if we introduce temperament and interaction styles before we address the preferences of the MBTI and Jung's cognitive processes. Consequently, by the time our participants encounter the cognitive processes, they are already close to selecting a best-fit type pattern through the use of temperament, interaction styles and MBTI results.

We have not found any way to start the self-discovery process using either the letters of the code or Jung's concepts to reliably get the "aha" experience of, "This is me!" People tend to tune in to a single process or preference in isolation, and miss the rest of what the code represents. We have years of examples of people identifying with a letter from the code because they scored it on the MBTI and then ignoring self-identification on any other dimension because they now "know" what type they are.

In addition to the goal of helping individuals identify their best-fit, we have a goal of helping them better understand how they function. We hope also to provide them with a powerful tool for growth and development.

Nouns or Verbs? Types or Processes?

A great deal of confusion results from talking about the cognitive processes as if they are nouns. When people are described as "sensors," "intuitors," "thinkers," or "feelers," it's as if that is all they are. In contrast, Jung described the processes and then described how an individual would act if they had that process as dominant in their personality. He indicated that everyone *can* use each of the processes, but are predisposed to more often use only two of the eight. Processes depict actions and are therefore better described with action verbs. Thus, we suggest "sensing," "intuiting," "thinking," or "feeling,"

and descriptors such as "while engaging the thinking process," or "as part of our experience while sensing."

Jung's concept of eight types is valuable and contributes a great deal to our understanding of personality by helping us distinguish which types are which. But it is not consistent with Jung's theory to talk about Thinking Types, for example, when referring to any type code with T in it—half of these type codes hold Thinking as a process (dominant or auxiliary) and therefore don't fully match Jung's general descriptions. In describing each whole type pattern, clearly indicate more than the presence of a single process as represented by a letter designation in the type code.

The Brief Descriptions

While our descriptions of the learning and problem-solving styles strongly reflect the cognitive processes, they were not "built" using a formula or by simply combining all the characteristics of the processes. They are based on the themes of each of the sixteen types as a whole. Jung described eight psychological types as characterized by their dominant process. We have chosen to honor the influences of other aspects of the patterns, such as temperament, interaction styles, and whole type themes in the development of our brief descriptions for the following reasons:

1. The unguided reader needs to resonate with the descriptions, so we kept them as rich and full as possible.

2. Each cognitive process "looks" different based on where it falls in the type pattern's hierarchy, so a "formula" description cannot portray accurate likeness.

Extraversion-Introversion

You may wonder why there is little emphasis on the extraversion-introversion dichotomy. As I worked with type concepts over the years, I kept noticing that what people attributed to the E-I difference reflected which cognitive process was being extraverted or introverted rather than a general attitude of E or I. When I went back to read *Psychological Types*, I realized that while Jung described the general attitudes of extraversion and introversion as central to his theory, his emphasis was on the processes.

> The hypothesis of introversion and extraversion allows us, first of all, to distinguish two large groups of psychological individuals. Yet this grouping is of such a superficial and general nature that it permits no more than this very general distinction . . . . If, therefore, we wish to determine wherein lie the differences between individuals belonging to a definite group, we must take a further step.*

---

* Carl G. Jung, *Psychological Types* (Princeton, N.J., Princeton University Press, 1995), 6.

This is not to say the E-I dichotomy is unimportant. It is simply not where we start when introducing this material. And we found it can contribute to perpetuating stereotypes that are counterproductive. (We do cover the essential E-I characteristic of Initiating-Responding in Interaction Styles.)

Important Differences

We found that in helping people determine their best-fit type, we had to be clear about how unalike the cognitive processes are when used in the introverted and extraverted attitudes. For example, the more we described Feeling as a process, the more we began describing either F_e or F_i, thus perplexing people about their own experience. Not attending to this confusion leads to stereotypes like, "I'm an ISTJ and I have no Feeling," when in truth there is often much evidence of F_i (loyalty, strong beliefs, and values) in most ISTJs, but descriptions of Feeling tend to portray the warmth and expressiveness of F_e.

Hierarchy of Functions

Jung suggested a hierarchy of functions and used the terms dominant, auxiliary, and inferior. Myers clarified and expanded on Jung's work in that area. Her interpretation of Jung was that the dominant took one attitude (extraverted or introverted), and the remaining processes took the opposite attitude. Subsequently, there has been a shift to depict the processes as balancing each other in terms of attitude. In other words, if the dominant is an extraverted perceiving process (S_e or N_e), then the inferior should be an introverted perceiving process. In this example, the auxiliary would be an introverted judging process (T_i or F_i), and the tertiary would be an extraverted judging process. This is the model we have adopted, as it best mirrors our observations. The following chart displays comparisons of the terms and functions used in each model using ENTJ as an example. It includes Beebe's archetypes and our roles of the processes.

The Heirarchy of Processes For an ENTJ			
Jung	**Myers**	**Beebe**	**Berens**
1st T_e Dominant	T_e Dominant	T_e Hero/Heroine	T_e + Leading / − Dominating
2nd N_i Auxiliary	N_i Auxiliary	N_i Good Parent	N_i + Supporting / − Overprotective
3rd S_i Tertiary	S_i Tertiary	S_e Puer/Puella	S_e + Relief / − Unsettling
4th F_i Inferior	F_i Inferior	F_i Anima/Animus	F_i + Aspirational / − Projective
5th		T_i Opposing Personality	T_i − Opposing / + Backup
6th		N_e Senex/Witch	N_e − Critical / + Discovery
7th		S_i Trickster	S_i − Deceiving / + Comedic
8th		F_e Demon/Daemon	F_e − Devilish / + Transformative

Tips for Clarifying Type

• Understand that when a process is used in the leading or supporting roles, it is often engaged automatically. When a different process is engaged, it may feel unusual and people are inclined to notice it and thus report that as their preference. A currently developing process will be uppermost in our minds and then it becomes our focus, rather than the inherent one.

• After introducing the cognitive processes, ask people to talk to each other. We often suggest they talk with someone who holds one of their less preferred processes as a leading or supporting process to learn how they express differently and to see how that process operates in its more positive aspect.

• If you have them work through the activities in this booklet, be sure to allow time for reflection; and some people will prefer to interact with others while doing activities.

• Remember that the processes are never used in isolation, but always within the pattern and in interaction.

We hope you find this booklet helpful for your own understanding and in your work. Please contact us at: training@tri-network.com with any comments or questions you have about this booklet.

Foundations of Temperament

Kretschmer, Ernst. *Physique and Character*. London: Harcourt Brace, 1925.

Roback, A. A. *The Psychology of Character*. New York: Arno Press, [1927] 1973.

Spränger, E. *Types of Men*. New York: Johnson Reprint Company, [1928] 1966.

More about Temperament

Berens, Linda V. "A Comparison of Jungian Function Theory and Keirseyan Temperament Theory in the Use of the Myers-Briggs Type Indicator." Doctoral dissertation, United States International University, 1985. Abstract in *Dissertation Abstracts International* (1986).

* Berens, Linda V. *Understanding Yourself and Others: An Introduction to Temperament*. Huntington Beach, Calif.: Telos Publications, 1998.

Choiniere, Ray, and David Keirsey. *Presidential Temperament*. Del Mar, Calif.: Prometheus Nemesis Books, 1992.

Delunas, Eve. *Survival Games Personalities Play*. Carmel, Calif.: SunInk Publications., 1992.

Keirsey, David. *Portraits of Temperament*. Del Mar, Calif.: Prometheus Nemesis Books, 1987.

Keirsey, David, and Marilyn Bates. *Please Understand Me*. 3d edition. Del Mar, Calif.: Prometheus Nemesis Books, 1978.

* Keirsey, David. *Please Understand Me II*. Del Mar, Calif.: Prometheus Nemesis Books, 1998.

The Sixteen Personality Types

* Baron, Renee. *What Type Am I?* New York: Penguin Putnam, 1998.

* Berens, Linda V., and Dario Nardi. *The 16 Personality Types: Descriptions for Self-Discovery*. Huntington Beach, Calif.: Telos Publications, 1999.

Berens, Linda V., and Olaf Isachsen. *A Quick Guide to Working Together with the Sixteen Types*. Huntington Beach, Calif.: Telos Publications, 1992.

* Brownsword, Alan W. *It Takes All Types!*. Nicasio, Calif.: HRM Press, 1987.

* Fairhurst, Alice M., and Lisa L. Fairhurst. *Effective Teaching, Effective Learning*. Palo Alto, Calif.: Consulting Psychologists Press, Inc., 1995.

* Isachsen, Olaf, and Linda V. Berens. *Working Together: A Personality Centered Approach to Management*. 3d edition. San Juan Capistrano, Calif.: Institute for Management Development, 1991.

* Nardi, Dario, *Character and Personality Type: Discovering Your Uniqueness for Career and Relationship Success*. Huntington Beach, Calif.: Telos Publications, 1999.

* Tieger, Paul D., and Barbara Barron-Tieger. *Do What You Are*. Boston, Mass.: Little, Brown and Company, 1995.

* Tieger, Paul D., and Barbara Barron-Tieger. *Nurture by Nature*. Boston, Mass.: Little, Brown and Company, 1997.

Jung/Myers Model

Brownsword, Alan W. *Psychological Type: An Introduction*. Nicasio, Calif.: HRM Press, 1989.

Harris, Anne Singer. *Living with Paradox*. Pacific Grove, Calif.: Brooks/Cole Publishing, 1996.

Jung, Carl G. *Psychological Types*. Princeton, N.J.: Princeton University Press, 1971.

Myers, Katharine and Linda Kirby. *Introduction to Type: Dynamics and Development*. Palo Alto, Calif.: Consulting Psychologists Press, 1995.

Myers, Isabel Briggs with Peter B. Myers. *Gifts Differing*. Palo Alto, Calif.: Consulting Psychologists Press, [1980] 1995.

Myers, Isabel Briggs; Mary H. McCaulley and Naomi L. Quenk. *MBTI Manual: A Guide to the Development and Use of the Myers-Briggs Type Indicator*. Palo Alto, Calif.: Consulting Psychologists Press, 1998.

Sharp, Daryl. *Personality Type, Jung's Model of Typology*. Toronto, Canada: Inner City Books, 1987.

Quenk, Naomi. *In the Grip*. Palo Alto, Calif.: Consulting Psychologists Press, 1985.

Systems Thinking

Bateson, Gregory. *Mind and Nature: A Necessary Unity*. New York: Bantam Books, 1979.

Bateson, Gregory. *Steps to an Ecology of Mind*. New York: Ballantine Books, 1972.

Capra, Fritjof. *The Web of Life*. New York: Anchor Books, Doubleday, 1996.

Oshry, Barry. *Seeing Systems: Unlocking the Mysteries of Organizational Life*. San Francisco, Calif.: Berrett-Koehler Publishers, 1996.

Wheatley, Margaret J. *Leadership and the New Science*. San Francisco, Calif.: Berrett-Koehler Publishers, 1992.

Wheatley, Margaret J., and Myron Kellner-Rogers. *A Simpler Way*. San Francisco, Calif.: Berrett-Koehler Publishers, 1996.

Biological Basis of Behavior

Ornstein, Robert. *The Roots of the Self: Unraveling the Mystery of Who We Are*. San Francisco: HarperCollins, 1993.

Hamer, Dean, and Peter Copeland. *Living with Our Genes: Why They Matter More Than You Think*. New York: Bantam Doubleday Dell, 1998.

Colt, George Howe. "Life Special: Were You Born That Way?" *Life* (April 1998): 38–50.

Cultural Influences

Hofstede, Geert. *Culture and Organizations: Software of the Mind*. New York: McGraw-Hill, 1997.

Learning

Knowles, Malcolm. *The Adult Learner*. Houston, Texas: Gulf Publishing, [1913] 1990.

Applying Multiple Models

Nardi, D., and L. Berens. "Wizards in the Wilderness and the Search for True Type." *Bulletin of Psychological Type* 21, no. 1 (1998). (This article is available on the Temperament Research Institute Web site—www.tri-network.com/articles)

On the Internet

Temperament Research Institute, www.tri-network.com

*Recommended for Beginners

Many of these products are available on the Temperament Research Institute website—**www.tri-network.com/catalog**